Managers Managing Magic: Enabling Creative Innovation

By Hywel Evans

For all managers everywhere who are trying their bloody best.

OPENING CREDITS

CUT TO <u>SCREENSHOT</u>

@(the author's twitter)
> I'm trying to write a book, explaining how creativity and innovation don't have to be either super processed, or crazy off the wall, but can be logical inventive + simple led by people's strengths. And your story pops up on 'late night Pixar'. Sums it all up perfectly.

@(Jessica Heidt - Script Supervisor at Pixar's Twitter -)
> Thank you so much!.. Nice! Best of luck with the book! Love the concept.

CUT TO <u>FILM CLIP</u>

PETER KAY: Thanks to Hywel and Jamie for holding it all together

CUT TO <u>WHATSAPP</u>

HYWEL'S DAD: Just make sure you point out at the start of the book that your ideas are just suggestions. You don't want people to lose their jobs because of you....

CUT TO <u>AUDIO CLIP</u>

LORD RICHARD ATTENBOROUGH*: Hywel, shut up a minute.

*see the very end of the book for a brief indulgent note about this wonderful man.

Running Order

Author's Note

This book is about understanding our thinking around creativity, to simply do things better - whatever that means for you, whether your aim is enhanced profit, improved user-experience, or increased staff retention / happiness. The word 'creativity' is stacked with problems and prejudice, which might initially make it feel unrelated to those aims.

When you say 'creativity' to people, many have an inbuilt reaction that ranges from, 'Wishy washy nonsense!' to,
'Ooh how exciting!' In both cases it is seen as something 'other' and often something to be a little cynical about or wary of.

This book does suggest a method or proactive 'recipe' for creativity at work. Largely because I know that a simple, step by step guide is something that is useful to many people. BUT the majority of the book is not primarily about telling you how to 'do creativity'. It is about understanding the complex origin story of our relationship with creativity, that brings forth those initial reactions of 'wishy washy' or 'special'. Creativity is neither of these things.

But let me take a shot at why we expect a creativity book to be like that. Many people have taken part in some kind of innovation 'event' at some point. One manager told me of a 'Next Big Idea' seminar, where the boss got everyone together for a day and told them to 'be more fish' (and other positive approaches from theories and books). They were essentially told to be creative for a day, and come up with the next big idea.

This is an incredibly difficult thing to do. Creativity is not something you can switch on for a day, otherwise we would all put aside a Saturday and come up with our million pound business idea. These kinds of events and approaches often lead to a sense of passive-aggressive pressure. Like being told to dance down the barrel of a gun.

This book is about understanding creativity properly, and what it is up against, so that you - the manager - can use the suggested method, interpreting it so that it fits into your workplace.

What it is here for is to help you to operate within the <u>real world</u> that you inhabit, and be able to ignite small, creative sparks that have the ability to take hold in your workforce. This is possible whether you work for Google, or you are in a prison cell. So unless you're somewhere worse than a prison cell, don't listen to the voice saying, 'But we're beyond hope.' Believe me, I've worked at some seriously bad places, for some seriously bad people, and creativity can grow in the darkest of spaces.

I'm on a mission to make people take creativity seriously, and it starts with you.

Six Short Creative Introductions

Tissues

Whilst writing this book I had a sudden flashback to something I had completely forgotten.

Age 6 or so. I was allergic to cats, and didn't figure this out until I went to university, when my permanently stuffed up and sneezy nose suddenly stopped, only to come back with a vengeance when I came home.

My twin brother and I slept in bunk beds with me on the top. I created a tunnel out of paper - like the chutes that drop down a building site to take rubble into the skip. Just like that. A miniature one, so I could blow my nose and drop the tissue down the pipe into the bin. Genius. However, it had not worked. Something had gone wrong, collapsed. I'd spent all day on this. I was so upset. It was after bedtime and I wrote a note to my mum and it said this, 'If I ever have an idea again, tell me to stop.' I ran into the living room with my hand over my mouth (because I was trying not to smile or cry, I'm not sure which) and threw the note at my mum, running out again and upstairs. A few minutes later my mum came into the room with her hand over her mouth and dropped a note on me. After she left I opened it and it said, 'Never stop having ideas. They are wonderful. Love mum'.

If my mum had helpfully written on the note, '*You see, the reason the tissue tube didn't work is that you used too much sellotape and the tube was too thin. I've done this study into tissues, and on average they are wider than......*' I would have probably drawn the conclusion that ideas were for smarter people than me, who do the research, already have the ability, or have other skills beyond me. And I would have given up. I probably wouldn't have gone on to try, fail, and succeed at so many things I've done ever since.

And yet, she could easily have thought that by engaging with me over the detail of the idea would have 'helped'. This is what we - you, me, your boss, your family members - do every day. We try to help, but we achieve the opposite. I want to explain why, and show how management within good creative processes, is exactly what my mum did.

She didn't engage with the idea. She engaged with the process. Why would you stop having ideas?

Isn't that amazing. I love my mum. What a nice thing to remember.

The Sad Truth About Most Ideas

Just beneath the ceiling of meeting rooms at night, everywhere around the world, from London to Lahore, Honolulu to Ho Chi Minh City, there is something sad happening.

Above the long table and strewn chairs, amid the fluorescent light that has been left on despite the energy saving directive on the wall, there are a million little ideas just floating amongst the dust particles, drifting in the air. Some have been there for years, some joined a few hours ago.

Their tiny faces are looking for their owner, but their owner went home. Because of things said in that room their owner lost their passion, love or interest in them, allowing the little idea to drift up in the air and join all of the other ideas that are gathered, left alone and waiting.

This ceiling is where ideas go to die.

I believe that we currently have a creativity crisis at a time when creativity is vital.

How many things have you wished you started, but didn't? How many things did you try once and then shelve? How many times have you felt an idea get shot down.

There is a question parents often ask me about creative pursuits. It's because a child has terrified them by suggesting they want to enrol on a creative course of some kind. They kind of nod or wink as they ask it as if they're asking me to tell the *real* truth, off the record.

'Nobody can really *teach* acting/directing/art can they?'

My answer used to be muddled. Now it is a straight forward, absolute, 'Yes.' There are as many methodologies, techniques and practices in art as there are in science, and you wouldn't ask, 'You can't *really* teach science can you?'

So What's This All About?

Well, I want you to imagine yourself in a movie for a moment, for an exciting scene.

INT. WORKPLACE. DAY.

You, the manager, at work.

Somebody is about to suggest a new idea. It might be they literally say, 'I have an idea!' or it could just be that you notice they are exploring using a new tool or method to do something old. Either way, you are about to open your mouth and say something to them…

PAUSE. You are frozen, as are they. Your mouth is   open, but before you have said anything we…

ZOOM inside the brain of the person in front of you, and we FLASH BACK in time through their entire life. We see a myriad of things happening to them that have affected their understanding of their ability to be 'creative'. Their school days, their attempts at starting new hobbies, their embarrassing moments standing in front of a group, EVERYTHING that leads up to this point.

ZOOM OUT to you and them on pause again.

You realise that the very next thing you say is not responding to the idea they have just had: it is also responding to all of those experiences and understandings.

You open your mouth to speak…

That's the moment that this whole book is about. Understanding how important the moment is, what's behind it, and how to respond in a way that works in all of the best creative industries I have witnessed.

Hyper-Creative

So who am I to talk to all these amazing managers and have the gumption (great word, underused) to think I can provide help with this? Maybe I can't! But if it's needed let me try and justify why my strange experience of 'work' is perhaps useful.

Much of my life - since the age of around eight - I have been involved in hyper-creative environments. 'Hyper-creative' is my best way of describing any role in which the job is to create something from nothing and deliver it every day. Literally starting with a blank page or an empty space that needs to be filled.

My CV, should I ever write one, would look something like this.

I have (*take a deep breath and read fast, or just skip the paragraph*)
Written plays and screenplays, tv pilots and adverts, been a script proofreader, a theatre director, ran Theatre In Education, am a University Visiting Lecturer in Radio, built and run a community radio station, successfully gaining an FM Broadcast licence, had a fifteen year career as a presenter on national and local radio, devised and produced comedy performances, created, developed and ultimately sold an advertising agency, acted, worked as an Enterprise Advisor with a large social housing organisation, Interviewed on live radio everyone from Lord Richard Attenborough to Harry Styles, been a talent scout, created a travel website, and lots of other things that started as an idea and, through helping others, became something tangible.

I also run a hotel for Rabbits.

I realised I might have a book to write, when I finally came to terms with the fact that this was quite an unusual way to spend a working life. It was only when someone called Jenny Chapman asked me a question about creativity that a million thoughts came to me at once and I realised for the first time that I'd spent my life understanding and managing the creative process, but had never been asked to pass that on consciously. I mean, I've been asked, 'How do I make a podcast?' but never, 'How do we become more creative?' Which is what Jenny asked.

I realised that it's really unusual for someone like me to actually be given that respect, to actually be *asked*: that creativity, or experience of operating a creative process, is rarely seen as what it is - a 'skill'.

Perhaps it's because of the history of work being a patriarchy, but we still talk in quite competitive and aggressive terms in work. 'Crossing the line'. 'Crushing the competition'. Sports metaphors are often used, and it's more likely a sport expert will be invited to consult or inspire than an artist or a clown. But why? Netflix, the BBC, the National Theatre are all places full of hard working dedicated people very much 'winning' at their business.

I wanted to find out where the cross-overs of creative processes occurred between those 'hyper creative' places and more traditional industries. So I began to talk to managers about creativity and innovation, and I came across that key moment I mentioned earlier. The moment when someone suggests an idea.

The nature of your response in this one tiny moment can mean the difference between the start of great things happening (and possibly lots of success or money for an organization) or the thwarting of potential positive change and improvement.

Now let's go to Hogwarts.

Protego Maxima! (Your Creative Mission by reading this book)

In the final film of the *Harry Potter* series, Professor McGonagall leads the staff in a spell which is cast around Hogwarts school.

"Protego Maxima!"

A massive forcefield is gradually created by everybody working together, and Hogwarts is put into a huge bubble which will protect, for a while, against the evil forces attacking it. Shots bounce off it; the enemy cannot run into it; it is protected.

So, too, creativity forms a protective charm around organisations which enable it. By innovating, the organisation stays fresh and competitive. By allowing individual thought, we encourage employees to stay. By a *culture of possibility* existing, negative elements of established medium and large organisations are replaced by feelings of excitement and adventure. A place, quite simply, where people want to be - whether they work there or use it, as customers.

But that can only happen when a similar protective charm is first cast around the initial idea. And try as we might, we are not doing a great job of this...

Shouting at Rabbits

I mentioned I run a hotel for rabbits. This is true. Let's not go into it now.

If you've ever tried to catch or chase a prey animal, like a chicken, rabbit, hamster, pigeon, you'll know that the worst thing you can do is make a lot of noise and run towards it, shouting at it to jump up into your arms like a dog.

The best thing you can do is very, very little. Just positioning yourself in the right place, making one noise at the right time, not scaring it too much and encouraging it to go in the direction you want. It only happens when you behave knowing that you might not catch it at all.

You are lucky to catch it. Your best chance is to proceed gently.

Creative ideas are prey animals. We can be complete, bumbling, cumbersome fools, who clod in like a toddler when we spot one. We pile on strategy or plans, deadlines or prescriptions, expectations, pressure and criticisms, questions, critiques, judgements, comparisons, systems and theories and goals!

That rabbit is gone. The hamster is down the back of the fridge. The pigeon flew off a few minutes ago. Or at least is on the roof deciding to move to the neighbours.

-

Managers often forget the simplest fact, that no matter how good, kind, friendly, relaxed, empowering you are, your employee always knows that you 'hold the gun'. You have the power to remove their livelihood. They are almost always in a state of self-conscious behaviour which is far from the creative state we feel when we are free.

Rabbits, when unafraid, are spectacular. Have you ever seen a rabbit leap in happiness? (If you haven't, youtube 'rabbit binky' and have the best time on YouTube you'll have this week.)

When we feel that nobody is watching or judging and there are no high stakes, we tend to become like that - comfortable and playful, naturally able to express things.

But you may now be thinking, 'I DO NOT HAVE TIME TO LEARN HOW TO BE GENTLE.' I know, you're a serious, seriously busy, manager, constantly fire-fighting. But I'm not talking a big bunch of hippy nonsense.

If you think of it not as 'time spent on ideas', but **'time spent on the things which will make us hugely successful, change the world, possibly rich, or happy'**, then it becomes just as serious as putting out those daily fires.

So if it's all that serious, what are we up against? And how can we bypass that barrier?

Welcome to the book!

PART ONE

Why We Kill Creativity

Introduction

When somebody points out a kind of prejudice that you were not aware of, you begin to notice it everywhere.

That's what this section is about. Sharing the understanding of what creativity is up against every single day, in lots of tiny and huge, practical and psychological ways. That the biggest - in fact only - enemy to our creativity is ourselves.

Starting with our most reliable in-built adversary...

We Don't Do Things That Way Here

How necessary regulation forms a behaviour beyond just
the regulation
How keeping only things that can be traditionally
measured excludes creativity
How this thinking becomes cultural - the person adopts
the behaviour of the self-preservation systems.

Russell, an actor friend of mine, went to work at a Japanese production line factory for two weeks. The goal, for the factory, was to finish the production of a new product for a large order, within fourteen days. Russell, however, is a pain in the arse. He is naturally creative and is used to doing jobs that are engaging - enjoyable - for the people doing them. So within a couple of days he was asking friends on the production line if they would like to swap jobs here and there. It soon started to happen that one person would swap places with another, three times a day, and as a result everyone was much less bored carrying out a variety of actions per day.

The foreman of the factory realised this was happening, and - acting as a translator for the Japanese management who were present - had to grill Russell as to why he was doing this.

'You don't understand,'said the managers. 'You are being less productive because every time people change roles they have to get up to speed and we have a lag in production.'

'Ah yes,' said Russell in his best stage voice, "we will lose time at first, getting the expertise in each task, but we will, eventually move even faster because we are happy.'

The managers spoke to each other in Japanese for a while, then the translation came back. 'OK, but if you are not finished in two weeks you will work overtime to finish the job, unpaid.'

21

They finished the entire production two days early, and had two days paid, in the pub.

First up, let's acknowledge that 'compliance' is really important and protects us. I'm not going to attack the concept of compliance or the wonderful people who keep me safe by working hard at it every day.

But the hidden truth is that many hold on more tightly than they need, to the belief that compliance is inflexible. Sometimes it is, and that's fine, but studies have shown that it takes a 'belief' that things cannot be changed, rather than the reality - that often there is flexibility. In the creation of safe compliance there's the danger of an equal and opposite reaction, which can land on the head of creativity.

As a business grows so do its systems. And the longer these exist, the more second-nature and ingrained they are. The very nature of 'new ideas' is at the very least a concept of something 'other' and 'to be introduced'. Like the arrival of a new animal to a socialised pack.

The individuals in the 'pack' have learned from the systems and operate within them, and their own reaction to new things mirrors that of the system. So rather than the 'computer saying no' the person does, and we believe intuitively that this is correct - that it protects us. 'No', objection, or caution is the first port of call.

This forms an inherent system-preservation-motive which has grown from the start and is now firmly in control. The bigger the organisation gets, the stronger that force. Collectively people block innovation because 'doing something better' often means saving money or time which in turn makes people fear for their jobs.

However, I want to argue that getting in the way of creativity, is actually more likely to increase the chance of job losses. Because ultimately, new ideas could mean agility in the marketplace, new inventions, more customers and engendering more need for employees. Without it you stand still and begin to lose, potentially resulting in job losses.

A few years ago many organisations accidentally or on-purpose doubled down the pressure on creativity through the same kind of logic that makes compliance 'rule'.

The banking crash in 2007/8 led to bosses streamlining and cutting back in areas perceived to be disposable - a process often driven by accountants and spreadsheets. What was frequently lost in places that did this badly, was the most valuable component, people, because their value couldn't always be measured. A super simple example (but one I witnessed with a real person) would be making redundant a receptionist who had worked somewhere for thirty years, and was the life and soul of the place. She made every customer feel valued and welcome and embodied what the company's heart was about. But she was thought to be too well paid for that role, having been there so long, and so was made redundant. These people who show love and soul within an organisation, are usually the ones who do so because they care the most. And If they care they are also most likely to be suggesting improvements and innovations - adding value both in making the place a pleasant environment but also with practical new ideas.

Some of these organisations have never recovered because they removed hearts when they thought they were removing superfluous waste. A management approach characterised by 'what can't be measured can't be managed' is a difficult one to reconcile with any attempt to value the intangible contributions like love and support that people make in an organisation, to the benefit of staff and customers. Unfortunately, the output of a well defined system is so much easier to calculate than the less tangible benefits of latent creativity.

Another cultural habit that is often developed in compliance-heavy organisations is at best 'risk averse'. Sometimes 'surprise averse'. They are either being supremely cautious about risk, or - as a result of that caution - trying to pre-empt everything. Perhaps there is a meeting where people of varying seniority are present, including a manager and a member of their staff. If that staff member suggests something new, they could be reprimanded after the meeting. 'Don't surprise me like that again. I wasn't expecting that suggestion.' This is a common side-effect of compliance-heavy places, and it literally encourages people to keep their mouth closed with regards to new things. This approach militates against fostering a creative environment.

Compliance is there to protect us but can also make us stay within rigid confines.

Compliance in hyper-creative places often requires only the adherence to a clear set of safety guidelines. The use of a sports hall, rehearsal space, practice studio for music or radio production will demand that we obey the venue's rules and regulations.

But you'll notice in each of these environments, where talented people are exercising their skills, they each have - literally - a marked out space. A place to exercise the talents and inventiveness of the people taking part. This space with freedom for play, is key to enabling creativity and we will return to it later when I describe my 'method'.

So compliance itself doesn't stop creativity. It requires people to hold on too tightly to it and use it as a reason why they THINK they cannot do something new.

Respect for creativity is often hard to find...

'Ladies and Gentlemen this is your pilot speaking, we have a serious situation, is there a Dancer on board?'

We are all prejudiced against creativity. You may think that you are not. But simply take part in this test. *Your child tells you that they are considering two options: being a lawyer or a clown.*

John C Reily (*Stepbrothers, Wreck It Ralph*), Eric Stonestreet ('Cam' from *Modern Family*) and Carey Grant (Carey Grant) trained as clowns or acrobats. Their 'net worth' ranges from 23 to 60 million dollars each.

I know so many people who went to drama or art school or something equally intense, who are now better paid, happier, and more successful than many of those who went and did a 'proper' degree.

But the chances are that if you met me and I told you I was a professor of microbiology, you would hold me in higher esteem than if I told you the truth - I went to drama school.

Why? I don't respect a history graduate more than I do a plumber. These things are different, and you can have a talented or untalented person in both.

Here's why.

Our education system was created to meet the needs of the industrial revolution, all modern mass education systems around the world began around that time. Before then, most kids were not guaranteed an education. Once industry boomed and factories needed huge workforces, there was a need for children to learn basic skills.

Factories were the destination, needing people to fill the gaps between the automated new machines of metal and steam. This meant teaching the young mind to follow orders very reliably, and so teaching would be a binary style: There is a right answer, for which you get praise, and a wrong answer for which you get punished. Lever A will turn apparatus B, which will produce C. Which lever turned B? A is correct. Well done. Praise. Get a question wrong and be scolded. Step out of line with the larger binary school rules, and receive corporal punishment. Today known as physical abuse.

What is the correct answer to the question, 'How does the colour purple make you feel?'' or 'What is a new mathematical discovery?'

There is no room for innovative (new) or creative and artistic thinking in an education system that was literally built on physical abuse when children got things 'wrong'.

And where today's curriculum is concerned, I know what is inside your head... I know that there is a hierarchy in your mind which says that the most important subjects were maths and science, and the least important were the arts.

A young child with what's considered too much energy is likely to be diagnosed with   a condition such as Attention Deficit Hyperactivity Disorder (ADHD) and prescribed medication to calm them down. Diagnosis aside, such children would rarely, if ever, also be 'prescribed' an activity to tap into their energetic selves, such as taking part in a dance class. Sir Ken Robinson spent a lifetime investigating, explaining and promoting the latter, and some of the people inspired by his work are now running schools adopting alternative, creative educational methods, often with incredible results. Certainly, for the individual children concerned, seeing the perceived problem from a different angle meant a lifeline to a flourishing new direction. Sir Ken's *Ted Talk* has been watched around seventy thousand times a day for the last decade on YouTube. It is called 'Do Schools Kill Creativity?' and if you have never watched it, you're in for a real treat. It's the most watched Ted Talk of all time, and it made me cry when I first watched it because it was the first time somebody had made sense of why I had felt like apologising for being creative my whole life. The same reason, I think, that it has been watched so much. Because everyone in the world who goes through the education system built for 'testing' feels a great sense of justice and clarity when they hear him describe it. A real therapy for the world.

Why we don't let teachers use their magic

This is not to attack teaching at all.

Teachers are magicians in my eyes. Most of my family and much of my extended family are teachers. They work with endlessly complex and regularly changing systems and syllabuses, targets and milestones, lesson plans and inclusion plans, and often look after hundreds of kids. There are so many wonderful teachers who are highly creative in how they teach. But often that creative thinking is not what they are passing on... Those creative powers are being used to unlock the same riddle everywhere... To find ever more interesting ways to focus the kids to get the 'right' answers - 'teaching to the test'.

I've seen teachers hand out the ten possible answers on the exam, a lengthy document on 'how to explain' each of the ten, and even numerous examples of literally what to write. Under 18's are praying for photographic memories so that they can remember all the answers that have been given to them. As targets are put on targets, syllabuses arrive and change in a whirlwind of league tables and postcodes, parents and promises, the teachers, clambering for breath under cutbacks and skeleton staff, try to make learning the answers as entertaining as possible. Because they HAVE to get the kids to pass.

The endgame is still the same as one hundred years ago. Teach what is correct, and pass.

<u>Taught out of thinking</u>

By the time they reach university age (when, as a visiting lecturer, I come across them), they are so used to having been shown how to do everything, that they are totally lost when asked to be creative. Students have asked me, 'How long does it have to be?' in answer to almost any open, creative challenge I've given them. My answer is always the same, 'As long as it is good.' This terrifies them. Because all of a sudden the marker, the measure, is a subjective opinion, and even more terrifying - it is THEIRS. The idea that they could create something using their own judgement as the measure is bizarre.

And it's not just on a creative course like the one I teach. In the 1990s, the Singapore Government became concerned that although its school leavers were obtaining superb examination results, the future economy required far more creative and innovative thinking by the next generation of business recruits. They decided to introduce courses in the sixth form or equivalent which taught students to think for themselves as well as pass the examinations.

The word 'crisis' is used a lot, but I suggest we do have a crisis in terms of a 'creative thinking drought'. Conspiracy theories and false heroes who pedal lies appear to be supremely attractive to young people. I would argue that this is, in part at least, because they have been made so creatively bored and numb elsewhere. The alternative answer has become incredibly appealing because their educators have, their entire life, been telling them the answer rather than asking them to seek one or invent one for themselves.

I asked a student of mine why they found it so hard to come up with new ideas. The answer was illuminating and sad.

'We are expected to be on the right side of everything. Whatever the latest campaign trying to change the world, from MeToo to TransRights, we have to be very careful about everything we say because it will be on social media, or somebody might put it on for us. And while we are trying so hard to get everything right, walking on a minefield, politics is showing us that all the mean bad guys who are anti all of those campaigns, are the ones in power. So we feel like we can say nothing, and when we do it's pointless. It's entirely depressing.'

Attending university or college, or whatever you did when you were 19-21, used to be a time of personal reinvention. Now I see students conforming desperately through fear of it being shot down, or of public humiliation.

It is the worst news for creativity if this pressure means that only the ideas that already exist are being voiced.

And adults are in exactly the same boat - we're all performing perfect visions of ourselves online every day. I'm 40 years old and can remember a time before social media where embarrassing things stay as blurred memories. Not any more! It's all being recorded, kids.

We all went through this system of learning to conform for the formative years of our life. From the way we are tested to the reduced importance of arts subjects in the 'hierarchy' and we are wired to think of 'new ideas' as 'wishy washy' and peripheral.

So now I'll really test your inbuilt prejudice. Try not to smirk at this...

Inside Drama School

If I were to pick one thing from drama school that, in a vacuum, you would think the most extreme, 'silly' example of creativity at work, it would be that I spent a term as a penguin.

This was as part of a 'movement' class called Animal Study. The class had to go to London Zoo, choose an animal, and work out its movements and how to imitate it. The idea is that most people walk in ways similar to different animals - some move sleekly like cats, some are heavy and plodding like hippos, and so on. (It's a good game next time you're people watching). Actors use this a lot to play parts. If they're playing a sneaky character they might have worked on the physicality by thinking about or studying snakes. Our bodies are very awkward and embarrassed, and it's not enough to just learn the lines for a part. Actors have to think about how this looks on the stage or screen, and give their body instructions about how to move. So animal study is widely used.

I was on the Directing course and this module was a preliminary way of understanding the acting process. It meant a roomful of awkward and unfit people wandering around like leopards or, in my case, penguins. So it was pretty funny. But that seemingly pointless or silly endeavour is taken absolutely seriously. It is tried, tested, and will have been used in front of you - by a millionaire performer in a film or a show on your TV in your living room.

The very nature of creativity being the formation of something - like a newborn baby - means that it is weaker, less solid, and therefore easily harmed and easily belittled. It is too easy for people not to see the wood for the trees. People being penguins without the logic of how it works, is an easy thing to criticise.

The problem is that people actually tend not to come knocking on that penguin-room door with *malice*. Nobody is the enemy! They come knocking with something far kinder and do it entirely innocently. They come with helpful criticism.

Hell-bent on Destruction

In a world hellbent on destruction, do not just critique. Create! Create! Create!

Alok

Vaid-Menon

At Netflix - one of my favourite companies to reference because of their revolutionary approach to most things - they actually reject the idea of protecting criticism. They dismiss something I believe in strongly which is that criticism should come when invited. The truth, as I see it, is that if you are working at Netflix with the absolute top creative minds - most highly sought after and highly paid experienced professionals - at the act of 'being creative', then yes, throw criticism around as much as you like. Everyone there has a wealth of similar experience and language to be able to do so without harm. But most organisations are not Netflix. They are not, by nature, experts at making TV, film, and entertainment which are environments that have decades of experience in how to give incredibly valuable feedback at the right time and in the right way. If I were to go and work for the England football team, having never played football or followed football much for my entire life, and I started giving the players my advice, I'm pretty sure it would not be helpful.

If we use an average human lifetime as a metaphor for 'creative' or 'new' ideas coming to fruition, I'd say they need to be left free of criticism until they are a teenager. In most organisations we stifle ideas as soon as, or before, they are born, with 'helpful' criticism.

32

You may be thinking...

A)   I only criticise bad ideas
B)   I only offer helpful advice from my experience
C)   I don't stifle

But
A)   How do you know?
B)   How do you know?
C)   How do you know?

Nobody is guilt free in this. It is what we do. Think of the last time this happened in a meeting at work...

Someone in the room says, 'I've got this idea to do X', and the very next thing to happen is an opinion is given. Often multiple opinions and a debate. Why? Because it FEELS a) polite and b) like we are paid to do so. Talking and giving 'constructive criticism' feels right on both a moral and employment basis. Especially if you are a manager.

Yet giving any answer that in any way judges a new idea, potentially stifles future success. And yes, even if the idea seems dreadful.

Imagine we show *Star Wars* to a focus group of people who have never seen that film. Every person in that focus group talks with absolute authority about what they think. Our opinions are solid and honest aren't they? You like tomatoes or you don't.

Here are some comments we might hear from the focus group.

'I don't like the space stuff.'

'I don't like the men in white suits.'

'I can't see the face of the guy in the black helmet and it's annoying.'

'I like the stuff with the furry guy who talks funny.'

If these comments had been listened to, it would not have turned out to be a multi billion dollar, probably hundred year franchise.

The problem we have is that within any team of people we act as that focus group.

Now imagine that the focus group is made up of people you respect, get on with, or even pay your wages. Not a bunch of strangers filling in surveys. People who have the power to hurt our feelings, or who we wish to please. The chance of that idea remaining protected from others, or your own confidence, is now minimal. The idea no longer belongs to you, it belongs to this imagined committee that you have to try and please.

So many ideas are abandoned at this point.

If we are the one criticising, the truth is that our judgement isn't even that reliable. I've been proven wrong a million times by things that appeared to be bad ideas at first. Something I am editing for a radio drama can sound dreadful one day, and the exact same clip can sound great the next. Our opinions are not fixed, they are fluid and easily biased by a myriad of things ranging from what we think of the person having the idea, our relationship with the subject in question, our imagination about what is being suggested, what we had for breakfast or how much sleep we had last night.

At work, when people try something creative, the manager, trying to help, has that conditioned urge to give an instant opinion. But the idea has just been born.

YOU ARE NOT A VILLAIN. ARE YOU?

We all do this critiquing. So why do we? We are not evil! We are absolutely unaware that we are doing it. Why?

Because whether we think we can provide well delivered considered feedback, or we like to 'say it as it is' or 'shoot from the hip', we are simply trying to HELP. If the idea appears good we get excited and want to get involved. If it appears awful, we want to 'nip it in the bud', or offer critique to help improve it. Sometimes we're between the two and think the idea 'potentially has some legs' but we try to assist in its building.

If you're thinking of that colleague who spouts terrible ideas all the time, or other examples of when someone has had a patently awful and laughable idea, just consider the route that all ideas take.

That black and white footage of the first attempts at air flight is hilarious. Fools flapping big wooden wings off the end of piers into the sea. Anyone in their right mind would look at them and say that humans flying is a completely stupid and embarassing waste of time. It's an extreme example, but rarely do I see an idea that doesn't look vastly different after the creator's first few iterations or attempts, which is why they must be allowed to reach that point. unimpeded by well meaning interventions.

It takes a long, hard, honest look at ourselves to realise that our best intentions, the useful comment we think we are making, is actually the easy bit. That is our ego saying, 'I am useful and intelligent and this person can be helped by me.' Truthfully, *anyone* can point that out. A child can point at that black and white footage and say, 'That won't fly.' The hard, adult, difficult thing to do is learn to say nothing - at first.

What our intervention achieves is to put a full stop and discouragement at the feet of the one who has been brave enough to bring forward an idea, no matter how right or wrong we may be. There is very rarely no such a thing as a bad idea early on: it just hasn't developed yet. So stopping it achieves nothing even though we think we are helping.

SELF CRITICISM

Forget about external criticism and just think of the internal voice that also forms a judgement.

It is a voice that we listen to more and more because we are getting impatient. We are consumers who are used to everything being perfect - being able to have things in their perfect form 'on a plate' within 'internet speed'.

We have to know that inside ourselves, or inside the minds of your colleagues, is a huge need to be patient.

When we look at something new we have created and instantly hate it, write it off, or discard it, it is often because our *skill* does not yet match our *taste*. Let me explain....

It takes years to become good at being a radio presenter. Our skill is developed over hundreds of hours on air. But it's likely that we wanted to be a radio presenter because we were already a fan of radio. So when we first open our mouths on a microphone for the first time, we already have a developed taste in radio. We could be experts. So then we sit and listen back to the recording of our first attempt at radio presenting and we are horrified. We 'hate the sound of our own voice', we - unfairly - compare what we hear on that recording to our favourite experienced professionals and we draw the conclusion that we are hopeless at it, and should never do it again.

Our skills in the practice have not had time to catch up with our refined taste as a consumer. So we flick the channel on our own attempts at new things, because we instantly judge them compared to established creations.

With ideas it is the same. We have a picture in our mind of what we want to do, and at the first attempt we look at it and say, 'Well, that's not what I imagined.' Our taste has criticised our skill, before it has had a chance to develop.

This psychology remains throughout the invention or testing of a new idea, and many people fall at the first hurdle and give up.

In a *good* (not all are good!) hyper-creative business, rather than criticise, ideas are tried out immediately - jump on your feet and 'show me' what you're thinking. If anybody does criticise, it is building upon the original idea, and this again only happens in a place where you can IMMEDIATELY try out their new version. At that point, you get up and do it. If it works, great, but the proof is in the pudding. And even within that rehearsal space there is a real understanding about who gives criticism and when.

There is also a strict and understood schedule to criticism in good hyper-creative places. The rehearsal of a musical will go on for weeks until anyone who can be classed as 'the money' can watch a run through. It is about the right criticism at the right time.

Here is a supremely simple, childlike example, which we all may have experienced though we're too old to remember.

A child is building a sandcastle. She asks for advice. 'What do you think my castle needs?' The adult says, 'A moat would be nice.' The child has asked for ideas, has taken it, and builds a moat - or feels free to reject it. 'I don't want a moat.' In the same situation a child doesn't ask for advice and an adult says, 'Hi. That castle doesn't have a moat.' The child was focussed on making some windows in the towers she had built. But now thinks her castle won't be proper until it has a moat. So she builds a moat. But now the windows still aren't finished, and the castle collapses when the tide comes in. She's a little dejected on the car ride home. 'It was a lovely castle,' says the adult. She says, 'Thank you.' But she knows it stopped being her castle when she got the uninvited architect.

So, dear manager, when Bob comes up with a new idea not only do you have to hold back your own criticism of a new idea, but you have to look after Bob too in the early stages of him trying to make it work.

One more quick note on 'criticism'.

Look out for the person who prides themselves on 'being outspoken'. You know who I'm talking about. The one that makes everyone take a sharp breath in. The ones who wear a 'candour badge' saying, 'Oh, you know me, I say what I think all the time.'

Candour is often confused with being 'helpfully honest'. Candour is perfect when given from one team member to another - two people building the same thing together. But outside of this very safe equal footing, it can be dangerous for self esteem. Whilst it's often respected and even thanked by those on the receiving end, underneath they feel shot to pieces.

Yes, there are times in high-pressure, fast-deadline, situations when very swift judgement calls are to be made, and Mr or Ms 'Candid' can blaze a trail through the emergency. That has nothing to do with the moment of someone floating a new idea, and they often whip out their 'candid sniper' at these moments too.

Which brings us nicely to what we tend to do before even opening our mouths and facing that potential criticism...

Thinking to Death: to get on with it, or not to get on with it. There is no question.

The use of 'thinking' as an excuse for 'inaction'
A simple 'don't think, just try' story

The whole point of Shakespeare's _Hamlet_ is 'What value is there in procrastination?' Hamlet takes about 3.5 hours of theatre time, to eventually get round to avenging his father's murder - i.e., the thing he's been banging on about for hours. And although, indeed, he does get around to the murder he's been planning, he ends up getting killed himself. Also his mother, and one of his ex-mates, also get killed. All within a few seconds. He really should have got on with it sooner or just shut up about it. The planning didn't help the outcome.

One of the most disappointing things I hear regularly is somebody saying, 'I'll give it some thought', or 'I'll do some more thinking.' These are often a shorthand for, 'You won't hear from me again.'

Just like there are red flags you look for in other processes, listen out for those phrases because they are a red flag of the creative process.

If you ask someone how they're getting on with an idea and they say they've been doing a lot of thinking, suggest that they get it out of their head and onto paper or into whatever the reality of their idea might be: whether it's woodwork, a spreadsheet, research, whatever the physical version of 'starting' is. It's incredibly valuable to turn it into a real physical thing rather than a mental exercise.

People say to me, 'You always seem to be very proactive and get things done!' yet when I talk to them about _their_ ideas it ends at, 'I'll give that some thought.'

We think that 'thinking' is 'doing' and it's not.

A Quick Story About Rabbits

We're on our honeymoon in Hawaii. Sitting on the runway ready to leave Honolulu airport, with the palm trees and turquoise sea outside, I ask Sarah why on earth we are leaving. It seems as sensible to me as pairing socks (pointless hours of life spent matching shins). She doesn't have an answer. So I ask what she would do if she could do anything at all. She says, 'Run a rabbit sanctuary.' Three days later at home I say, 'Come on then. By the time we go to bed….' And we open the garage and pull out all the horrible dead spiders and bits of rubbish in there. An old 1940's garage. In good nick, but needing some insulation and bits and bobs. [Much later you'll hear me talk about "the sacred space" - a place where ideas are tried out - in hindsight this was ours.]

With absolutely no tested, requisite skills, we went to the DIY store and bought what we thought we needed. Garage cleared out completely, we went to a couple of garden centres the next day and bought some hutches. Hey presto. We have a rabbit sanctuary.

Over the first few months we found ourselves signing up more and more people who wanted to board their rabbits while going on holiday, the 'sanctuary' side of it was more difficult and less demand. Within two months of Hawaii we were fully booked, and since then we haven't looked back. We have expanded the business, replaced the old garage with twelve barn-style cabins, and we could fill the place twice over in summer and at Christmas with regular customers.

We had an idea, we entered the space and we had a go, and we learned a lot. The money it makes us has taken us back to Hawaii a few times since.

It isn't that we are supremely talented at rabbit-sitting. It is that, of all the people who may be having the same 'thought', we simply 'Did'. So it's fine for people to 'think' about their ideas, but an idea sitting in someone's head ruminating without any trial or practicality is still, in reality, nothing.

I know so many people who talk a good talk, for years, about doing something. Their thinking often goes straight to a finished picture that involves a huge amount of money, investment or time. And so no action begins.

For example, if you were to be thinking about starting a cake shop, you could have built the perfect shop-front in your head, and the perfect 'cupcake menu'. But years later, even though the menu has been extended and the shop front is even more colourful, not a single cake has been baked or offered to a friend to taste. Soon, the image of the shop and the imagined taste of the menu, will begin to lose colour, wilt and die.

Without actually turning on a blender, baking some cakes, and asking people to try them, you have done as much as I am now imagining my perfect castle on a cloud, with a unicorn standing on the ramparts. No I was never a fan of *My Little Pony*, but it is my imagined castle and my imagined unicorn alright!

When people finally begin to 'do' something, they often fall into a different deadly trap... Instead of baking a cake, they, instead reach for a blank pad and write at the top Business Plan.

Planning the Life out of it

Why our belief in planning helps us fail
How planning can blinker us from new ideas
Why hedging your bets is the hyper-creative method

Ewan, a six year old, decided he wanted to fly. So he strapped the sides of a Welsh-dresser to his arms and leapt off the garage roof. Observers say he lifted slightly before he hit the ground. Which, to Ewan, made the broken arm more than worth it. A true story.

I'm on Ewan's side.

When somebody does bring you an idea, they may have done a lot of thinking beforehand. Those who don't bring ideas forward are likely to have over thought or over planned and decided not to come at all. We'll look at idea generation (encouraging new ideas) later. But right now let's look at how we naturally think that we can over-plan our way out of potential failure, and inadvertently move ourselves closer to the failure we are trying to avoid.

You may have heard this statistic before.

'Up to 90% of new businesses fail within the first year.'

So building a business is very dangerous and difficult. We presume.

It's an example of one of many myths around creativity and self-starting. We are made to feel it's hugely difficult, hugely important, and the stakes are really high. Have you got a friend who's a painter and decorator? Does that person really look like they've been on *The Apprentice* and had to walk through the fires of hell in order to take the huge risk of self-employment? Probably not. In fact, you might feel a little envious at their contentment, freedom and autonomy.

In fact, that statistic can give us the wrong impression. The businesses that often fail in this 90% include the big money people - investment bankers - who have decided to buy a huge, fancy, posh restaurant, putting a million pounds in, and tried to succeed quickly. Most of us don't have a million pounds to throw at something, so most of the data behind the statistic doesn't really involve people like us.

The fear we have around starting enterprises of any kind, leads us to think that we need a huge plan. Well thought-out business planning. Or, in the case of suggesting something new at work, a really good detailed case that you've formed in your head, alone, using lots of impressive ideas and stats.

Education led us to believe that if we follow the trail of breadcrumbs, we will find the bread. (Research, find the answer, get the answer right). But new ideas don't exist yet! There is no bread to be searched for. So if you're following a trail, you're certainly not heading for *your* idea. You're on the wrong path! The planning is leading you either somewhere that is not original, or it is a lie - you are heading nowhere. Those millionaires with their restaurants followed 'the plan'. It failed because following there is no set plan for success, even with a lot of money. (Otherwise Mcdonalds would have long-since been replaced by the next trillionaire who wants to sell burgers).

Business planning, before actually starting, involves so much guesswork. Anyone can project that in year one of my business I'll find a million customers - probably miles away from reality - rather than just focussing on business planning at a desk with a spreadsheet, trying ideas out in a sandbox or actually meeting users - trying, converting, listening, talking to potential customers or users.

But even taking that approach, life and ideas don't always work like that. A friend of mine is an incredible planner. He is a businessman who has started more than one successful business, and he really is an uber example of analysing the plan ahead. He moves very carefully. His first business, however, like many successful ventures, didn't begin with a plan; it began with him as a teenager playing with computers and servers, and his business grew from that. Retrospectively, he couldn't have planned which of his hobbies, one of which was as a singer in a band, would take off.

As I was writing this chapter I shared a draft with him. He sent me a message, which perhaps shows how the idea tends to lead the way rather than the plan.

Haha! One of the things I've learned over time is to embrace the chaos of moving forward. Still a recovering perfectionist, but learned from experience and others that the best approach is to start, then carry on.
We built a software system for work for which I had this neat idea for a feature around which it would all be centred. I spent ages designing it etc. In the process I ended up adding a few incidental features around the edges. We then started using and the incidental features ended up being most useful and the things that we use day in day out now, the central feature I originally envisaged is now mothballed as it was neat in theory but rarely used in real life. Now we don't develop any new features on the system until we have used them as a paper or manual process first. Lesson learned.

In professional creative environments this is precisely how it works - you only EVER decide what works by doing it. In creative pursuits, you have maybe ten drafts or versions, and you pick the best pieces.

'Pilot Season' in America is when TV networks launch a bunch of 'first episodes' of a series. They are waiting to see which of them is most likely to succeed before commissioning any more episodes. Creative success actually requires the acceptance of a great deal of what you might perceive as 'failure' - the nine out of ten shows that aren't picked up, perhaps.

So beware the person who holds a big plan, or who is doing a great deal of pre-planning before actually starting. Creativity is often killed by the over planning of a single idea, rather than the simple starting and 'playing' with ten ideas - and seeing which one takes off.

Watch them or they'll cheat

Why mistrusting staff costs a lot more
Why over-prescriptive management causes misery
How micromanagement doesn't work in hyper-creative
environments

I recently spoke to someone who works for an organisation very different from the one I'm now lucky enough to work for. During the coronavirus pandemic many organisations had to find a way of trusting people in work. But this person said to me that all managers and their staff had to send an email at 9.01am just to prove they were online. Each boss checking up on their team.

This is Command and Control writ large, and it is unfortunately very common.

Let's be kind for a moment, to this poor managerial soul, and say that their intentions are good. By taking measures such as these they are presumably aiming for more profit and/or productivity, which keeps everyone in a job. The ship won't sink.

However, the resulting, unintended consequences of managerial interventions like this are likely to cost more in the longer term and reduce productivity. It's highly likely that the email at 9.01 is counterproductive. Perhaps they include in the content of their email the suggestion of a pointless meeting of some kind, or other invented smoke-screen 'work'. People will spend time at that meeting - hours of time used up. It's also likely to make the member of staff feel completely untrusted, treated like a child, and prompt them, at 9.02, to get on a jobs website looking for a better place to work.

Just consider the extra hours of 'pretend work' this creates because the person has begun to hate the organisation that doesn't trust them. The HR Department spends time and money employing new, replacement staff, who may be less skilled, requiring additional training to familiarise them with the organisation.

The alternative is trusting staff, treating them as adults and hoping that they will move towards innovation and adjustments in order to deal with crises such as the pandemic, possibly giving birth to new approaches and ways of working that build profit, outcomes AND trust in the organisation.

In my organisation the chief executive actively told people not to feel obliged to work a rigid schedule they had been used to before the pandemic. The work needed to be done - there was no reduction in expectation there - but she said, '...Don't work to the old in-house schedule! If you need to deal with the stress, work when you can, spend time with the family, smell the roses, go for a walk, watch TV, work when you can in a way that works best for you.'

People responded to the positive and supportive message received. They worked at different times in different ways. It caused productivity to increase. Those in I.T. reported a huge spike in people logging in out of hours, working at times that suited them, and doing more. Being treated like an adult triggered a sense of loyalty and gratitude from the staff. I have every confidence that it will also be shown in staff retention.

There are plenty of organisations where people at the top give unnecessarily prescriptive orders. In theatre, there have been some very 'command and control' directors over the years. I used to be fascinated by the pictures of a Russian theatre director called Meyerhold. He could have a hundred people onstage, every one of them doing something extremely specific, forming a perfect picture - a little like ballet. I loved the pictures. I was almost drawn to the idea of micro-'direction', to tell everyone what to do down to the split second. I also worked with a great Russian director, who said to me, 'Yes, you might like Meyerhold, but you have to understand that he comes from years of hard oppression.' Her point was that culturally this kind of 'perfection' was achieved through a regime of fierce orders, misery for those involved, and a modus operandi of stifling individuality.

Managers have vastly different styles, and when you read the above, and how you react to it, will probably tell you where you sit on the spectrum of 'work when you can' to 'send an email at 9.01'. The closer to the latter you are, the more 'command and control' you are likely to favour and the more likely you are to find your staff frustrated when it comes to wanting them to 'get involved' with new ideas or new suggestions from yourself. If everything comes from you, they will be unsure what to do when asked to think for themselves.

You can make a very tightly-run, safe ship with command and control, but it will be at the expense of allowing for creative thinking. In creativity the real magic comes when people are having fun and being playful. Why is Monty Python so good? Yes, the stars have brains and a script, concepts, direction, and skills. But the performers are friends and within their performing is an element of joy and inventiveness that you can see at home when siblings mess around. In creativity, command and control actually does not work very well. It *can*, but you're missing the best stuff.

Going for Silver. Every Time.

Choosing to come a 'steady second' can be a conscious
strategy for some
An OFSTED example
Even Disney needed to think as an individual

After Walt Disney had years of ground-breaking success and acclaim as a fastidious and obsessive leader of 'artists making the greatest art possible', he made his company 'public'. i.e., controlled by a board rather than him alone.

The new-look company started to make films much less perfect than those Walt had previously made. Shareholder logic, and perceived 'safe moves' were harming the company's success.

Meanwhile, a miserable Walt began a new project of which he was solely and secretively in charge. He took some staff to one side and began working on a little idea based around a model railroad.

That railroad became the train that circled the model of 'Disneyland'. Its success and the success of all the sister parks and 'worlds' that followed is, one can truly say, a fairy tale come true. Especially for the shareholders.

He began it all 'off radar' with talented people in a building on the Disney lot. By returning to a pursuit of the 'best' the parks became a hugely successful saviour, and inspiration to rescue the film side of the business.

Yes, restrictive systems limit creativity. But a further danger is that in some contexts there's a more deliberate and conscious decision which keeps new ideas reigned in. This isn't about the natural results of compliance; this is an actual conscious decision to limit people's ability to think for themselves.

There are of course parts of organisations, such as car assembly lines or safety requirements in potential or actual dangerous work contexts, where adhering to the system's manual is crucial for the quality of the product or the safety of staff and customers. But even here the best firms allow for staff who have the direct experience on the front line, to feed in their suggestions, and explore adjustments or alternatives which might then be built into the system. Sadly, some less forward looking places are happy to limit themselves by opting for what they see as a secure second best.

OFSTED inspects schools and colleges to help parents and students know how well these institutions are doing and to encourage further improvement. An inspector once explained to me an example of the essential differences between an 'outstanding' grade 1 and a 'good' grade 2. Some places simply would never be able to get above a 2 as long as their leader was still there, stubbornly holding on to the same tried and tested methods.

In this case that leader had decided that every lesson plan should follow a checklist of what was deemed to make good practice. This was regardless of whether the full checklist was appropriate for that lesson.

'Use of I.T.' was on the checklist. In many lessons, most obviously Music and Art, there is absolutely no need to use I.T. But submitting a lesson plan to your boss without it, was interpreted as 'not allowed'.

Why? These leaders thought that slavishly including these prerequisites on all lesson plans meant that inspectors would say, 'Yep, really good lessons, ticking all the boxes.' However, what mattered more to inspectors, as it did to students, was the quality of teaching actually being delivered. How well the students were enabled to learn. But even with this pointed out, the leader here stuck to their system because, even though a grade 2 resulted, they felt the staff and lessons were controllable - nothing was left to chance and there would be no hostages to fortune.

Coming first always involves some uncontrollable magic, some element of risk. Of course, coming first may be something you're not interested in competitively - but I'm still talking about allowing people to feel flexible and open to new ideas. The same is true with getting a 'first' at university degree level. The difference between that and a 2:1 can, for example, be the inclusion of some new perspective which is relevant but not necessarily part of the orthodox approach to the subject - something the marker is impressed by that it really does stand out in its quality. Not necessarily splitting the atom or writing Beethoven's Fifth but demonstrating some new understanding of the subject which gives others confidence to explore new perspectives. As someone who marks university modules, I can tell you that it's obvious when you see it. Because it's the same reaction you have when you watch a truly great TV show or film. You stand back and say, 'Wow, I've had my eyes opened!' or 'How did they do that!' or 'You've moved me and I'm not sure how.'

So, although it's understandable to want a 'steady ship', it can be perilous.

In radio, this mistake was made by some big players who had market domination. It happened also with Blockbuster video, and Kodak, and many others. When the world changed they did not adapt fast enough. They continued to operate in the same way they always had. Some radio stations, for example, carried on running the same shows, the same way of selling adverts, the same routine, as their competitors destroyed them with increasingly high listening figures. They carried on because they were still making profit - keep the system going, just make more cutbacks! It may be a purposeful choice to keep to the same steady course, but if you are slowly sinking, hindsight may suggest that the really good creative space where you could have been able to adapt your strategy was a better option after all.

If this atrophy is happening to your organisation it likely comes from the very top, and changing it is extremely difficult. However, you very likely still have some power as a manager over the way your team works.

An investment of a small amount of time could well be worthwhile to work on ideas before you take them to more senior decision makers in the organisation and make a case for them being profitable or successful.

Which finally brings us from all of the things that creativity has to face, and on to what you are going to do, in order to enable creativity within or around you.

PART TWO

What you will enable

Introduction

A story...

Matt Damon is sitting on Mars, and he is starving. He's managed to grow potatoes. He picks up a book and reads to himself. It says...

'I've really tried hard in this book not to use atmospheric and flora and fungi type analogies, but now I really feel like I have to, and so I've decided to make it more exciting by using Matt Damon and Potatoes.'

Matt turns the page. It continues.

'Matt will soon grow a crop of potatoes - spoiler alert - in the movie he is in, called *The Martian*. The reason it is so amazing, is that Mars does not have an atmosphere that would support growing life of any kind. He has to cobble together a lab within his little space station using plastic sheets, old doors, oxygen, water, his own faeces, a bunsen burner, and some other things that I don't understand.

By reading this book by Hywel Evans, Matt Damon, you will be able to not just grow potatoes but also ideas - creativity - if your staff ever find their way back to you and you don't die alone on Mars.

Because, Matt, you and all managers are smart, intelligent, charming and good looking people, you will interpret this whole book in your own way. Which is why it's so important to understand what you are going to enable. What you actually are going to use to help create the perfect idea-growing atmosphere.

And Matthew, it won't be soil or oxygen. There will be other elements. The elements of Chaos, Ownership, Inspiration and Servitude. Sounds confusing? Oh come on, compared to growing a spud anything does. Grow up man. Read on.'

Trust in Chaos

Ron Howard (*Happy Days* actor, now Director of many great films like *Apollo Thirteen*) tells a story that when making a film with Tom Hanks, Tom was trying some things out on camera that Ron thought was crazy - out there - too comedic. Trying to control the chaos in the space in front of him, he asked Tom to reign it in. Tom reigned it in.

When Ron reached the editing phase of production he realised that what Tom had been doing was perfect from the audience's viewpoint.

Since that day, he has a 'thought rule' for himself, and his little rule is 'WWTHD' ('What would Tom Hanks do?') which he applies every time an actor experiments in a way he feels is against his plan.

When a colleague asks to work on something - in the method I describe later - you will allow them to go away and try things out - play around a little. It is against much of your 'better judgement' to not try to find out what's happening in that room, but to keep your distance. The more you allow this early on in creativity, the more positive surprises you may discover. Without the space or the trust, people cannot find that which does not exist yet. Ideas. Ideas come out of Chaos so we have to get a grip with the feeling of letting it go.

If you're worried about the idea of chaos, remember that fear of chaos is more often than not unwarranted. It isn't in the nature of people to want to create chaos. If you've ever come across a dead set of traffic lights, you'll know that people manage to make it work. Mostly. People move towards social order and working together. So 'chaos' can often be fear of something that most organisations have never even seen, just mitigate against.

Standing by a river you don't know what's in the water, how fast, how deep, or what's coming downstream. I'd argue a river is chaotic. It also, however, has the guidance of the bank and the forces pulling the water. For the purposes of this section, think of yourself as the river's guide - the river bank, if you like - but accept the possibility of chaos within your guidance.

And chaos as a concept has helped those who have found different ways of actively allowing it. Let's consider Netflix. I'm not encouraging copying what another company does - yours is different; but they are a great example of how *conceptually* they embraced the idea of chaos.

At the very start of their journey Netflix recognised that the bigger a company becomes, the more systems are needed. Netflix also figured that the bigger a company becomes, the more time and money is spent running these systems - and that they potentially squash creativity and growth. So they came up with a crazy idea. They said, 'The bigger we get the more systems we will REMOVE.'

They then said, as you are now imagining, that this would create CHAOS. And the way they would counterbalance this chaos was to employ even better people who could think for themselves and love what they do.

For example, most places have a system that means staff can book holiday days - vacation days - leave etc. You probably log on to a system, fill in a form, submit it to the manager, who then reviews and approves it, which gets checked by someone in HR, and you get the go-ahead for your days off. Imagine you remove that system. CHAOS.

Not necessarily. If you work for Netflix, within minimal expectations such as being available for group meetings, you simply work when you want and don't work when you don't. Want a holiday? Fine. Your job is to get the work done. So it's unlikely, if you are someone who is right for the job, that you will schedule any time that will harm your work. You are trusted and empowered to make it work. And for Netflix it does. I don't advocate simply lifting things that work elsewhere and placing them in your workplace, as I know work scheduling is so crucial in many organisations to keep production running and deploy staff efficiently - but by taking Netflix's philosophy and exploring ways of applying it or a modification of it, to your own team could be more possible than you think. It goes back to 'the way we've always done things' compared to thinking about how you would do things if there were a brand new design.

Specifically (for this book anyway) chaos is a useful concept when you're focussed on problem solving. As I said earlier, when you're innovating, one of the biggest blocks can be the picture in your own head of the finished product. You are trying to solve a problem and you begin to imagine what the solution is, so you work towards it. But you need to be flexible and accommodate possible amendments to that picture. If you're not building in *time and opportunity* for some *space and chaos* then you're being rigid. Better to allow people to experiment safely within defined parameters.

The method we will get to is the birth of that idea - being that river bank, offering some guidance - but allowing yourself to be entirely surprised by the controlled chaos within the river.

Enable Ownership

Why ownership is important and the alternative doesn't
work as well
Why sitting back and making suggestions is easy; why
innovation is hard

Some organisations do not ask their staff for ideas on how to improve.

Some organisations ask their staff for ideas on how to improve.

Some organisations ask their staff to improve things.

I have experienced all three of these approaches, and now firmly believe that the third is the best. There are lots of people who disagree with me. I'm going to try and make my case, and in doing so justify the way I'm going to suggest you enable ideas in the next part of the book. Because you are going to try to enable *ownership*.

When I say this to people they often disagree quite firmly. For two main reasons.
1. People on the front line can't be expected to enact change outside their power circle
and
2. it's not fair to ask people to do extra work - if the company wants extra hours they should pay for it.

I used to agree entirely with both of those sentences.

Bob is on the 'front line', he has to use company software which takes him forever to log into. He is offered the chance to provide feedback in a 'suggestions box' and he writes, 'Computer programme awful, takes too long, locks me out a lot.' He pops it in the suggestion box.

1.   Bob simply doesn't have the knowledge or power to replace the IT systems he is using; to suggest otherwise would be like asking me to sprout wings and fly.
2.   Bob's busy enough, we don't want him to waste hours on this when he should be servicing customers.

I cannot disagree with either of those things.

So people try to create a way of innovating that accepts these things as a 'given', almost invariably acting as follows...
1.   they send ideas to the experts - the IT department;
2.   everybody waits for the IT department to work on it.

But the I.T. department is also made up of people with busy jobs. And what happens is a strange stalemate of 'non-expectation expectation'. In other words everyone expects someone else to do it, but without really expecting anything to happen because they know everyone is busy.

The net result is quite simple. Things do not get done.

That is unless a scary senior boss is the friend of the person who came up with the idea, or in conversation whilst 'on the shop floor' somebody tells the senior boss about their idea.

The boss then says, 'That's great. Why isn't this happening?'

A chain of managers all flurry around sending emails asking everyone else why it wasn't done, and somebody ends up having to do it.

The person who does it never had the time in the first place of course.

So where do we end up? A few ideas get generated, due to the whim and pressure of a senior boss, and everybody else gets nowhere. The result being that generally the staff say, 'Yeah we try innovation but nothing gets done!' and the senior boss says, 'We need to be more innovative!' and tasks somebody with finding ideas, at which point a meeting happens and people go right back to the start and say, 'Well, obviously we can't expect people to work on the ideas themselves. They're too busy or not equipped.'

And the whole circle begins again.

So how could something work that allows for those two things - generating ideas in the first place, and enabling them to be worked on? Well, there's Google's 20% rule (staff spend one day a week working on whatever they want to work on, innovation-wise)...but hang on. That's individual ownership.

What if we employed ten people and THEY are the people with their time to work on things! Great. Yes?

Only what would happen is that those people would have to go to the front line, and work with the people who came up with the ideas anyway. So still ownership.

What people really want when they talk about innovation and those two problems is a world where they tell the company a problem, sit back and watch it get fixed. There are plenty of examples where that will be happening every day anyway. It's not like the I.T department aren't currently working hard on the next development to introduce. Whatever way you do it, someone will have to find the time. And in my experience, I've found that the *best* person to do that is the person who came up with the idea. Notice the italics on 'best'. That's my point: it may not be perfect, but the results speak for themselves. The best methods of innovating do not come from someone suggesting someone else does the work. They come from individuals choosing to take on an idea finding them.

So that is what you will be encouraging.

I am talking, of course, about the beginning of an idea. This whole book / 'system', is about looking after ideas at their early stages. After they have had a chance to develop a little and reach the point when a strong case can be made for them further 'up the tree', then they can be absorbed by more senior strategic people and, lo and behold, someone is being paid to work on the idea.

Other methods can and, of course, do work. I'm talking about what I believe and what, in my experience, works best. Small ownership that can grow.

Enable a Culture of Inspiration not Motivation

I am going to get up and go running tomorrow morning. Only I'm not. It will be cold, I will press snooze on my alarm, and snooze again, and it will be too late... My conclusion will be that I am fat and lazy and will have a Mcdonalds breakfast, whilst planning my run for tomorrow.

Rob Holman, author of *Lead the Way* offers a really great description of the two thoughts that motivate us into action. My interpretation follows.

MOTIVATED ACTION

Motivated action is what we frequently, mistakenly think ALL action requires.

Human beings, whether managers or not, think of anything difficult as needing 'motivation'. Like me running, or perhaps deciding to clean the house, or - in work - do the tasks we are least keen on. It's no surprise that when we then think of a new idea, a new task, or something creative we also then look to motivate ourselves. We tell ourselves to 'just get on with it'. 'Bite the bullet'. 'Drag yourself up by your bootstraps'. This is all well and good if you are talking about things you are paid to do - i.e. 'We must submit this work by this deadline.' But we're forgetting that the reason we're doing this is often quite negative - the fear of getting in trouble, causing damage, or not getting paid!

With new ideas, shouting at ourselves or others, simply does not work.

With anything 'new' this doesn't work because there is no externally set deadline, just the one we imagine for ourselves. The following promises are highly likely to NOT happen...

'I'll join Alcoholics Anonymous by November.'
'I'll paint my first painting by Sunday.'
'I'll sit down and write some great ideas before lunch.'

When we don't absolutely HAVE to drag ourselves through a difficult task, we put it off, we procrastinate, something else becomes much more important, and we simply do not start.

An externally driven task results in motivated action. It works when it is vital and there is pressure, but the experience of doing it is often unsatisfying, miserable, or lacklustre. You're likely to do what you're told, and do the bare minimum to 'get it done'.

INSPIRED

Whilst we think all action requires motivation, that's simply because we aren't noticing all the other things we're doing with our day.

What motivation do you need to press play on the tv show in which you are currently ensconced?

What motivation do you need to pick up your pet and give it a cuddle?

What motivation do you need to play your favourite song on your musical instrument?

None. That's because this kind of action is INSPIRED. It is easy, fun, and we often can't wait to do it.

Often, nowadays, people trying to quit an addiction are not given 'motivation' instruction, but instead are asked to imagine the wonderful things they will do tomorrow if they are not chained to their addiction. Inspired action.

Children are more likely to tidy their rooms if they want to be able to find something they really want to play with! Rather than if an adult tells them to do it. Inspired action.

We do things we look forward to taking part in - not the results initially. The marathon runner may delight in crossing the line, but who runs 26 miles in order to enjoy crossing a line? Why not 5, 15 or 50 miles? They enjoy the process of running, and that is why they do it.

Take writing this book for example. If somebody had told me I MUST write this book and it must be GREAT, I'd have struggled to drag myself through the process.

But I was INSPIRED by Jenny Chapman who asked me a question about creativity, which started me wondering whether to share my thoughts more widely. I WANTED to write a book, and I've worked for months until late at night, drafting and redrafting. I've enjoyed the actual process of sitting down and writing, rather than worrying about how good it is, or of pleasing somebody else, or of a deadline. Of course there are people I want to please by writing the book - namely YOU. But as a creative 'type' I have, for years, got used to pushing aside that thought knowing it will cause me to stumble. Instead I focus on the enjoyment of scribbling a new paragraph or honing a previous one.

Inspiration that encourages us to look forward to the process is invaluable. Motivation that ships us into crossing the finish line, will likely bring a miserable or lackluster journey. In the world of ideas, the 'inspired' process brings forward much more energy, commitment, and quality through its inherent *ownership*. In other words, if someone really looks forward to doing something, the results will be better than those who were frog marched in, during, and out of the process.

It has always been fascinating to me that in the entertainment world, the best show is always your last. When you leave one radio station for another, the final show you do absolutely crackles. The last night of the tour of a play is often electric. Everyone loves it. Why? Because the members of the team are not *motivating* themselves and thinking about every small step in order to 'get the job done'. They are not *worrying* about pleasing the boss, or clients, or the audience. They are inspired to create something that comes naturally, that they enjoy and that they think their audience will enjoy.

If you don't believe me, think about this. If tomorrow was your last ever day at work - if you knew you were leaving to go and get paid a great salary somewhere else, how easy would you find the day? How natural and fun would it be to just worry less and simply fly through whatever task you had to do?

So how do you encourage inspired action?

First, it's really difficult, because usually inspiration comes from a selfish thought, a personal love, or a desire unique to the person. (For example, not everyone will enjoy the same TV show you are watching: it's different for everyone).

With 'motivation' it's easy - which is why we default to it. You simply make a threat, offer a bribe or bonus and make them do it. 'Do this, or you'll get in trouble or lose out financially.'

With inspiration it is about finding the simple, individual thing that makes someone believe that the task is enjoyable. And it is much harder to 'hand' that to someone, than it is to encourage them to find it themself.

Here's an example. When I started one job I used to meet people in a windowless, grey, cold room. They would often not turn up, when they did it was dour, and I too felt miserable at the end of the day in that 'bunker'. One day I realised that I could meet people in a coffee shop instead. Selfishly of course, I loved the idea of being able to have a 'gingerbread latte' at work, but this selfish - inspirational - thought, was ok because it also had lots of positive reasons for the work itself: The coffee shop was easier for my customers to get to, it was bright, colourful, made almost entirely of windows, and the buzz in the place made everyone more relaxed - and, importantly, more creative. Within two weeks the difference was noticeable. I really wanted to get in the car and go to work early. Cancelled appointments with me were halved, and everyone was more productive in achieving what we were there to achieve.

If you feel stuck with a colleague who is 'not getting it done' in some way at the moment, it's likely you're trying to motivate them. Which means it may just need to get done. With new ideas, ask the person 'why' they want to do it, which drills down into the reason they personally wanted to take on this task. After that, ask them to feel free to enjoy it. Let them suggest the environment, the snacks, the music that they want. Make the process enjoyable. If this means providing ice cream - so be it!

Professional football has long been an industry of high salaries and bonuses to attract, retain and 'motivate' the best players. Managers in the past have been renowned for 'reading the riot act' and even allegedly hurling boots at players in the dressing room to admonish their performance. Of course, if high pay meant 'winning' then your team would never lose. This attempt at motivating action (through money and command) clearly did not mean a guaranteed perfect season of results. Recently, however, it was refreshing to see an interview with one of the most successful and inspirational managers in the Premier League, talking about his key message to his players before the game begins. He would tell them to enjoy playing the game. No threats, no promised retribution, just pure inspiration.

Rehearsal rooms in Hollywood are not full of actors wearing suits, uncomfortable, and terrified. They are in comfortable clothes, with shrieks of laughter, lots of their favourite avocados (or whatever Californians enjoy), and they work long and hard into the night.

The 'why' of us doing things is often, at their core, because at some point in the past we were highly passionate about it. The football team, and the actors, have been through years of 'love' for what they do. They may have grown out of it, as many of us do in 'passion' projects when they become routine. But the reminder of their 'why' is very easy. 'Go out and enjoy playing' is something they can easily tap into, and takes them back to a time before money and motivation was part of the equation.

There is nothing wrong with accepting that if something is not fun, people are less likely to do it. If you imagine that a task is 100% boring or routine and mundane, and you are able to add in aspects to get to 49% boring, you'll be moving towards inspired action.

For example, when I have to do a mandatory online course of some kind - health and safety training for example - I will try to turn it into something fun. I'll decide on a comfy chair, a pot of my favourite tea, and some favourite biscuits. Knowing this in advance makes me actually want to do it! Plus, vitally, I'm looking forward to the next one!

But encouraging creativity through inspiration can only happen when you actually allow people space to find new ideas, and that means taking a good hard look at how much attention you are giving to creating that space.

CAVE MANAGER

You may have heard the notion of 'busy work versus productive work', busy work being that which keeps us really busy but isn't really moving much forward, in contrast to productive work that generates positive results.

Usually when managing, we are doing a lot of busy work that involves making sure our team is serving the goals that we have been handed. However, because we have just got in the habit of how we do things, we can end up prioritising the busy rather than the productive.

As a manager it is possible to ask yourself a question to 'reset' what your fundamental role is by imagining you're the first manager ever.

The question is not, 'If you were the first manager ever, what would you do?' Because no early cave dweller ever decided one day to 'be a manager'. A manager would have been a necessity much later when society required several people to work together on tasks.

So the question is - if you WANTED a manager for the first time, what would you want them to do?

Let's go to the cave dwellers sitting around a fire. Two people cutting wood and putting it into the fire for warmth. If you're one of them, you don't need a manager.

If the village grew in numbers and there were a few people across a number of fires, spread apart, you might realise that there is a bit of competition for the wood-store, so you may try and organise… You need a helper. Someone who can keep an eye on the wood pile for both groups, and make sure everyone gets a share.

The manager is born of the need to support and enable the people doing the actual work.

The perfect manager is watching and enabling.

A theatre or film director, if they're any good, cannot be seen in their actors' performances. The actors are supremely confident, enabled to perform at their best, with their own take on their character after some collaborative advice from the director.

Steven Spielberg does not shout, bully or intimidate people. He enables them. Despite ALL of his years of work preparing for his story to come to life, he allows his employees to find their own passion and their own expression.
And don't underestimate Spielberg's calmness and niceness as a human being! Can you imagine a manager who could have as many millions - possibly billions - of dollars riding on their head, all that pressure, and still allow their staff to feel like they do when singing in the shower!

In business leadership, Ronald Heifetz (Harvard University) suggests that people are looking for someone who can give them three things.

Direction, Protection and Order.

Yet many managers spend their time largely on order - the busy work. Troubleshooting, micromanaging, approving, checking, distributing, making sure that everyone is where they should be with what they need at the right time.

The good news is that therein lies the secret. According to Heifetz, Direction, Protection and Order are the only three things that ALL people need to feel, for them to consider you a good manager. However, you're only a good manager if you can keep those three to a minimum. In so doing you create the space in which my suggested work can exist. You can find the time and space to do it, but you need to return to the basics and reduce anything that is the act of 'being busy' rather than 'being useful'.

Even if you were to consider your staff a bunch of absolute dummies who have no idea how to do their job, I promise you that imagining you are there to serve them and respect the latent ideas in their heads - that even they haven't found yet - will help everything to gradually improve.

Nurturing their idea will be one thing (the part after next); but first, the fun part. How do you actually encourage people to find an idea in their brain in the first place. How do you generate ideas?

PART THREE

Generating Ideas

Introduction

Tumbleweed.

Every manager in history, from Julias Caesar to Oprah Winfrey, will have experienced that moment, that gloriously awful moment, when they ask their staff to 'contribute' to ideas and there is nothing.

Except the sound of tumbleweed.

It's all well and good me tapping away on my keyboard here about how you are going to be able to enable creativity in that moment when a team member knocks on your door and says, 'I have an idea!' But that presumes there will *be* a knock.

Not just the sound of tumbleweed.

We have great expectations of people, and the tumbleweed moment is all the more painful when we feel we have really, REALLY tried to allow people some space to contribute. I hear it a lot. 'I got everyone together, asked them to speak, and nobody wanted to speak... I created a chat for people to come up with problems that need solving and nobody types in it.... I gave people a challenge and nobody rose to it.'

The problem in most of these cases is the word 'I'. You have tried your best to motivate, and it hasn't worked. Like a child being asked to clean their bedroom, actually achieving your desired result is as 'easy' as pulling teeth. However, when that child decides to clean their room themselves, it's a much better job, immaculate, and inspired.

So how to get people to your door with ideas. Here are a few simple things to try, to encourage the wonderful moment when the knock on the door or the email pops up with, 'I have an idea.'

Generating Through Workshops - the best way?

The mountain retreat
The useful workshop
The one to one invitation

Yes, there are plenty of workshops. But as one manager said to me recently, 'I don't think a 'mountain retreat' is always the best way of generating new ideas.' And I agree. Depending on the follow up. Often, it can lead to something that removes people from their current environment only to find that when they return to work, the ideas evaporate and we go back to business as usual. Sometimes it can be productive, and often more in a sense of a strategic learning exercise, or a team bonding 'away day'. But be aware that if the stated goal is to problem solve or come up with new ideas, you need to ensure the follow through. This often doesn't happen and what you've gained in terms of team building isn't worth its weight when compared to what you've lost in belief in the stated goals.

I regularly see a much greater return from individuals working on solo projects than from these big events.

I run sessions called 'Idea Generator' workshops which involve people finding ideas from their passions - thinking about work in the same way they do about hobbies. It has always, without fail, worked - every single person there, no matter how creative or uncreative they think they are, invents a new idea to work on.

In terms of group workshops, there can be value; but be aware that what you should avoid doing is just asking for 'feedback', which invariably results in a list of unobtainable 'moans' or 'gripes'. There is a place for, and a value in this kind of activity, but in my book (and this *is* my book) it is better to ask people to work in pairs or groups of friends in order to discuss actual, *new* ideas which they would like to explore *themselves*.

75

Following such exercises, simply announcing that your door is open and if anybody wishes to work on their ideas they can come and see you, is potentially a much better way of starting people off on their own journey and getting something useful from the away day scenario.

One way of encouraging ideas is to use the phone or talk face-to-face, one by one, rather than always defaulting to a big group email or announcement. By calling your team members one at a time and explaining to them that your door is open should they have a new idea, you are explicitly inviting new thoughts. But how you do this is often tricky and faces that difficult 'tumbleweed' moment when nothing comes forward from some people. (From others you might have ten ideas at once!) It may be that your reputation as a fierce manager who doesn't listen is deterring the knock on the door. In which case that in itself is a signal to try and change the way your staff perceive you as a manager.

The best thing to do is talk in real practical terms. 'Hi Jim. You know, when you're doing your work, if you feel like something you're doing is pointless, too long, or too complicated, and you have just the beginning of an idea of how to make that better, knock on my door. You don't have to have a full thought-out plan, just the start of an idea you might want to try out.'

Generating through a Positive Projection

During the Covid lockdown, I did an online course with Harvard University (Exercising Leadership: Foundational Principles). It was great fun and that's where I first heard a really good explanation of challenging the well-known theory that *we are afraid of change*.

People don't fear *change*, they fear *uncertainty*. If you are told that you've won the lottery, are you afraid of change? NOPE. But there's gonna be some bloody big changes, right?

What we are afraid of is the uncertainty that lives in the gap between where we are now, and the change itself. But only if we can't see what the change is. Now, we might not know exactly what we'll spend the lottery winnings on yet; we don't have a list. But we are not afraid of it because we think that this uncertainty will lead to great choices and positive change.

With creativity and innovation we have to deal with enough fear (for the reasons mentioned in part one), so be aware of how you pitch it to people. If you enter a workplace and say, 'We're going to look at making some changes!' you're likely to get back absolute fear. Avoid the change word. Everyone immediately knuckles down and tightens the screws on whatever their role is. Their tasks become essential, urgent, built in stone; they are eager to prove how important, how indispensable, they are.

Building the positive image of potential change is the goal. So saying something like, 'Let's try this, because if it works it might make everything you do easier.'

So many systems that cause stress and pain have the potential to be simplified or sidelined. Yet people hold on tight to them for protection even though they hate them and often don't see any positive benefit of them.

If you are going to innovate and be creative, you must allow people to really look forward to the future it is designed to create. Easier, better, happier. That way they are not afraid of risking anything within that gap between the idea of change, and the change itself. If, however, your aim is to reduce staff numbers as a result of this innovation - i.e., cost saving rather than cultural change - be wary of using innovation as the excuse. Redundancies are redundancies. If you brand them as innovation, you will turn that word toxic for anyone who stays and hears you mention it again!

Generating with the simplest question: a story about amazing Vicki

A true story about a manager who changed my world

This is a great technique that worked on me in terms of generating a passionate new focus and new idea.

Working as a radio presenter on a flagship breakfast show, my presenting partner Jamie, and I, had been getting amazing listening figures and were without a boss. (He had left abruptly, and that's another book). A new Sales boss came in, called Vicki Allison. A wonderful human being. She called a meeting with us and we expected to be told what the new strategy was, how we were to behave, that we should talk about hair-straighteners on air because our target audience was female. (A real quote we heard once.) But no. Vicki sat down with us in the studio after the show, and said, 'Love what you guys do. How can I help you?'

To which we took a breath and said 'What?'

She said, 'What do you want to do? How can I help you do it?'

I didn't miss another beat. This station with zero budget for anything related to programming (literally, no budget for marketing the shows, even buying pens, anything) was asking what we wanted to do. I said, 'I want to take the show to Las Vegas and broadcast from there for a week.'

She said, 'Great. How do we do that?'

What followed was the hardest I've ever worked in my life. The brief is this - get four people (two presenters, a producer and a newsreader) to Las Vegas for a week with zero budget, broadcasting live. Make it relevant to the people at home, and even try to make money with it for Sales.

I sent hundreds of emails, wrote stories, came up with files and files of audio that we would replace when there, so we had templates, planned trips to the Grand Canyon, Death Valley, Frank Sinatra's old lounge, packages that we would record and edit and play out during the live broadcast. I arranged a broadcast partner, a hotel with a studio in it, and a minute by minute plan for the whole team both away and at home for how it would all tie together...

Cut forward one year, and we had devised and implemented a long-running plot on air about us trying to get Jamie, dressed as Lionel Ritchie, on stage in Vegas as a tribute act. It started as gigs in workplaces in Preston, achieved its objective in Las Vegas, and came home, ending with a huge variety performance with talent from across the North West on stage in the theatre at the end of Blackpool's North Pier. It was like *Strictly Come Dancing* meets *Stars in their Eyes*, and the sponsorship that came with the whole thing got us free flights, hotel, and made about 40k for the station. It was an inclusive, local piece of radio that then won an award at the 'Oscars' of radio that year for 'Best Feature'. As we went up onstage to receive the award from 'Walking in the Air's' Aled Jones, I thought back to Vicki saying, 'How can I help you?' She didn't have to do a great deal, she just enabled us to work on something we really wanted to do, and got hours and hours of dedication, time, love, and money out of it.

Whether it is an arranged meeting or just a chat over a coffee in the kitchen, asking 'Tell me, how can I help you? What would you love to do?' can be a real way to get some ambitious ideas, find out problems, or just plant a seed of what you're open to hearing. It's incredibly simple, incredibly obvious, but incredibly rare to be asked such an open question from 'higher up the chain' and can be incredibly transformative.

Generating From Unique Perspective

Another true story that has changed the world

I urge you to watch the series of short (roughly ten minute) episodes of *'Inside Pixar'* on Disney Plus.

One episode is about a woman called Jessica Heidt who is Script Supervisor at the company. She is in charge of monitoring, tracking, and passing out every latest draft of a script to everyone on a production. An important and complex role.

She began to realise that the scripts were 'male heavy' in terms of characters, and she decided to start keeping a spreadsheet of all the characters Pixar included in their scripts.

She noticed that nobody was gender-biased on purpose, but as different departments made changes and cut characters, collectively there were always six males to four females, which over a cast of perhaps 200 is a huge difference in terms of who the world sees on screen. Girls throughout the world were seeing themselves represented as important parts of stories much less often than boys.

So she began to simply show the data to those who had any influence over scripts. She presented the data without any form of agenda, simply to show everyone the situation. Gradually, over time they reached a 50/50 split across all films, and now have gone further to represent a range of genders in their films. She also teamed up with a guy in the software department who created a computer programme that could do the work for her - scanning for names and gender. It is used across the industry, not just in Pixar. What started out as a small spreadsheet has transformed the industry.

The key feature of this story is the source of the initial idea. Jessica Heidt had a unique perspective - as we all do in our roles - and had the skills to assemble the evidence, develop her focus and the drive to present them to those who needed to get the message.

As she says in the documentary,

'If you're faced with a problem that seems bigger than you are, and you don't know what to do with it, take a step back and think about what specific tools you have that nobody else has. And I also just go ahead and do it. You gotta be fearless.'

Tell people this story, or show them the ten minute episode (Inside Pixar) and simply leave it at that. I guarantee someone will be inspired by it.

PART FOUR

HOW TO ENABLE

Introduction

Here we are. Finally at the 'recipe', the list of instructions, my advice to you about how to react when somebody says, 'I have an idea!' and what to do following that point.

It is based on a few years' experience with my colleague (boss), Eric. We are lucky in that we are employed to actually develop enterprising ideas. So what we have created is something called 'The Ideas Studio', which is a place where managers can actually send people to work with us on their idea. It is a safe space with us, impartial colleagues, who can help use our experience to guide people.

Most places do not have that luxury however, and even in our organisation we couldn't be responsible for ALL new ideas. (It's hard to create a 'culture' of creativity if every single creative thought has to be passed through two people). So it is down to managers to be able to get ideas to a certain point. So what is that point?

- **How to identify types of ideas**
- **What to do when an idea knocks on your door**
- **Ten steps to help an idea to grow**

The goal is to take the seed of an idea and get it to a small test. That's the goal. Beyond an initial 'safe test' there will then be lots more work required.

Within this system or method, one of the first things you will do when someone suggests an idea is to recognise what TYPE of idea this is, so I'm going to define some terms you may be aware of, to suggest how best I think you can triage ideas.

They are

1.   **Technical** problem based ideas
2.   **Adaptive** problem based ideas
3.   **Passion** based ideas

A **Technical** Problem is one which has an answer out there to be found. This could be a tool, software, something physical or digital, the point being that it already exists and just has to be found. Some time is going to be needed to find it, or find the best solution to your problem, but it's probably in existence already. Generally speaking, it is much easier to apply deadlines to technical problems...

'Ok team, we have a week to sift through X, Y and Z and find the answer.'

An **Adaptive** Problem is one which will require changes and/or learning, and might not have an answer at all. It's a journey that may fail, because we don't yet know the answer. Either that, or we're asking our team to learn new skills they've never used. People need to adapt to it, and the search for a solution needs to be open and flexible.

Some technical problems may already have a route 'in-house' to find the answers. For example, if someone couldn't operate their computer you wouldn't necessarily need to innovate - just call the I.T. Department for help.

With adaptive problems you can apply all the deadlines and pressure you like, but you won't necessarily gain anything other than an angry, miserable team.

'OK team, let's come up with the meaning of life by Tuesday lunchtime. Go!'

A **Passion-based Idea** is one that is entirely new and born of someone's imagination. It is not necessarily invented to solve a problem, though it hopefully will. It could be that somebody has an interest or hobby outside work and they think they could use it to create something of benefit within the workplace or for customers. Perhaps if someone said, 'I want to start an inter-departmental Olympics to help build team spirit.' Or someone realises that they have a skill that could be utilised somewhere: 'I do X as a hobby, and it could be something that could really help to deliver Y.' This, in a very small business, could be the invention of a new product.

With ideas formed from passion, a deadline might work but most are likely to be things that are new to you.

So let's do this. I'm going to try and compress it into a few simple paragraphs, so that the actual 'method' is there without justification. I'll then expand with the logic and detail.

THE MAGIC 'MOUTH SHUT, MIND OPEN' METHOD

Someone knocks on the door, you are busy working, or in conversation, and they tell you their idea.

Your brain will automatically want to respond to the idea. Don't. No matter how good, bad, exciting, or ludicrous the idea, offer no judgement, instead look at the human being in front of you.

1.   PRAISE.

Thank them or congratulate them, for being creative. As one manager said to me, 'I'd thank them for just making the effort to bring an idea forward.' Perfect. Ask them why they want to pursue the idea and you'll get them thinking about their passion for it. The story. Again, not to evaluate: just to get them thinking and say, 'Ok,' at the end.

2.   PROCESS.

Explain to them that when someone brings you an idea, you do the same thing every time - 'I don't comment on the idea because I want you to be the boss of this idea for now. I want you to explore the idea, and try to get to a test, a prototype, or an example.'

3.   PEOPLE

'In order to do this we'll set a time and place for you to work on it a little, and then come back to me. First of all, is there anyone you are working with on this, or anyone you'd like to buddy up with?'

4.   PLACE and TIME

Allocate them a very specific time slot to work on the idea, and tell them you don't want them to let anything else get in the way of this. You're giving them permission to spend Monday 3-5pm on this (for example). Ask them where they would like to do it. Completely up to them. It just has to be a specific place, and should preferably be a different environment i.e., not sitting next to you, not in the office surrounded by ears and eyes: it could be a meeting room or even the coffee shop or pub next door.

5.   PROJECT TYPE

Meanwhile you have been triaging in your head. Is this a TECHNICAL, ADAPTIVE, or PASSION project? If it is a technical problem that requires just a small amount of exploration you might even be able to set a deadline, so that the next meeting is when they've done the work and bring it to you. If it's a more complicated technical problem, an adaptive problem or passion idea, simply set the next meeting without any kind of deadline or pressure. What you anticipated might be a technical problem could turn out to be an adaptive one if no off-the-shelf solution can be found so you amend your strategy to cater for the adaptive approach

'So you'll work on it some more on Monday and bring me what you've got this time next week.' Set a meeting.

6.   PRESSURE

Take away as much pressure as possible. Remember, it's highly likely that many people will return having got nowhere, lost enthusiasm, and doubt themselves. So point out, 'If you come up with nothing, if you find yourself stuck, or if you do lots of work, we meet at that time anyway. It's not about how great the work is at this point, I'm simply giving you some time and space to work and then you can tell me more.'

7.   THE NEXT MEETING

If they return completely stuck, offer them advice on how to be creative - NOT on the idea itself still. Remember, you're wanting them to be solely responsible for their invention at this point. I list some examples of ways that people can jog the creative brain into action later in the book: you could use those.

- LOOP if needs be. Send them back to their time and place again and repeat the process until they reach a point where you can move on.

If they return with anything else - from what they think is a 'finished' idea, to a really strong development - describe to them the next step.

'We are aiming for a safe test. I want you to go away next and come up with a plan for that test. The two things you need to think about are
A)   how can you test the idea on one person or a very small number of people safely?
B)   how will you measure whether it works?

Give them an example. Here's a simple one.

'If we worked at an ice cream factory, and your idea was to create a new flavour, we would need to a) create one batch and b) get a focus group. The measure we might use is that we want more than 60% of the focus group to think the ice cream is great.'

So don't decide this with them, send them away to come up with their plan, and ask them to return and present it to you.

8.   PROTOTYPE

Again, at this stage if they haven't done what you asked, don't do it for them - get them to do it. But hopefully they return and you can finally offer some judgement! Not on the idea, again, but on the measures. If you think they have the measures too stringent or too soft, tell them, and agree on new ones.   At this point they may even need some money to afford the test. That's where you need to use either budgets or contacts to try and enable them to carry out their test. Arrange what you can, and again, set time and space aside for the test to take place.

9.   PRESENT for PERMISSION

If the test goes well, it's time to ask them to make whatever presentation you need, to take this further. Whatever the process might be in your organisation to get permission to roll something out with a larger budget, that's for you to wrangle with. Of course, you might be able to roll it out yourself and make it happen. But whatever happens...

10.   PRAISE (REGARDLESS OF RESULT)

Money isn't endless, and it's quite possible that an idea is great but gets a 'no'. There are lots of other reasons beyond money that may cause a no, too. You, yourself, may have this decision to make, and have to finally feed back to them on why you don't want to take it further. But by this point you will all have the same data. You will have decided the measures with them, and you will be able to justify why it won't be going any further.

If that is the case, it's likely they have seen it coming. But then often the decision is made by somebody else who simply can't be persuaded.

At this point, success or not, praise is the key thing. Creativity can be addictive, just like any adventure - travel, holidays etc. Some holidays are great, some are a washout. But you still get addicted to the trying. To the travel.

If they have a successful idea and you walk them into the office saying, 'Look at what Sarah did! She saved us £2000 with her great idea, so come on everyone, have an idea and bring it to me!' you will instantly scare off many people - because you are putting a value on ideas. In other words, stating that *success* is the point. Instead, whether someone succeeds or fails, say, 'Sarah brought an idea forward, she's worked on it loads, and she's been amazing. If you have an idea, please come forward because we LOVE working on new stuff.'

At any stage, you can use your own management style and judgement to adapt the method to best enable your staff to commit to it. So, if they DON'T meet at the time and place you agreed, then by all means be a manager and tell them you are disappointed - that they have not kept to the agreed arrangement. But never say this about the idea.

The Magician

Being a magician
How to create a 'Sacred space'
How to manage creative blocks

To those who took part in that ten step creative process, it should have appeared you really guided with a light touch and did very little. That's good!

The magician makes the trick look magic and simple.

So here is what you need to know, logic and tips, to help you deliver this simple approach.

What you are creating takes us way back to considering how hyper-creative organisations, even when working within compliance requirements/ rules, throw a protective ring around their creative space. Like Hogwarts, protected by a spell. This has been called, in theatre and not surprisingly, religion, '**The Sacred Space**'. In some of the earliest forms of story-telling, theatre, worship, sport there was literally a circle drawn in the sand where the action would be allowed to take place.

In all creative processes that I have observed, a version of this protected, 'sacred' space exits. It exists long before any kind of private or public performance. It begins at conception: a place for ideas to be played with. The spaces people work in creatively range from physical to digital to mobile. Writers write in offices, online together in teams via Skype or Zoom etc, or at various meeting points - coffee shops, parks, pubs... In all cases, the environment is earmarked and those invited into this environment are always - at first - the artists. NOT the critics, judges, audience, or leaders.

The Sacred Space

A quick practical example of the sacred space and why it's important that it's both sacred and a clearly defined space.

To a writer, an office or an attic or a shed is more important than a laptop on the knee on the couch.

I have written lots of things and heard interviews with lots of writers who say similar things to my own experience, which is that the most important thing you need to do to get something written is to commit to a time and a place of work, regardless of how well you think it's going, or the writer's block. 'I write between 8pm and midnight, no matter how good it is. I go to my office, I sit, and I write, and then I stop.'

It's so vital that the creative work isn't dictated by how well or badly you feel it's going. It's dictated by the discipline of being in that time and space . Some days lots will happen, some days little progress will be made, and some days emotionally you think it's awful. But the work gets slowly done.

The same is true in all hyper-creative environments - you meet, you rehearse or develop, and you make SOMETHING as a result.

A fixed half hour, hour, or afternoon, at regular appointment times is easiest to arrange of course. The space is up to you or the team who will be doing it. It could be virtual, physical, or acoustic even (audio - down the phone!) What's important is that it is a clear time and space that is sacred - it must not be interfered with in terms of 'more important things'. Because when you're dealing with an empty space, everything seems more important!

Deciding who goes into the space

The reason I encourage working in partners is that people with good working relationships can benefit from 'bouncing off each other' in the early stages. IF the person tells you they want to take someone else to work in the space, or if you're using the 'sacred space' idea to send people to work on ideas yourself, remember that working with friends is really OK at this early stage. It is often seen as a negative 'silo' effect. But actually at this point in idea creation, whatever makes people feel more comfortable with the project and able to express themselves is a plus.

Be aware of what gets taken into the space

Remember the business plans? Some people are really addicted to stacks of research and paper. It may work for them but if it's group work we're talking about, it can very quickly become a rod for their own back. Try to notice if people are over-planning or if other contributors start to join the process and turn up with something that looks like a predetermined, finished picture for the actual work. Additional ideas are fine of course, but especially look out for people saying, 'Ok, I know how this will work because I've seen it done over here.'

Alarm bells should ring. I've seen many a great idea be railroaded into a mediocre idea, because somebody thinks they've already got the blueprint sorted. If they do, send them off alone to make a prototype or do it themselves. I would guess pretty firmly that if you're in the mode of 'innovation' it isn't because you already have the answers!

Structure, around the formation of ideas, is acceptable. Predetermined plans that are certain of success are usually flawed. (Otherwise, everyone would be a millionaire because they could find the solution on Google).

Decide the basic rules - if any are needed

You really shouldn't have to tell adults many basic rules to take with them when they work creatively.   But the most obvious rule to have in a workplace is...

-        come up with ideas and work on them in private, safely, within the law and without interfering with current outward-facing practice. Keep it in the lab!

Any other rules should only be absolutely necessary. But I would suggest one more key one.

-        Only criticise if you can build.

One of my heroes who, in his lifetime, took over the world with his entertainment, was Jim Henson of *The Muppets*. Henson was essentially a hippy, who knew how to create as a genius. But one understanding was that if someone made a joke to use, the only acceptable criticism of that joke was to make a funnier joke. The same is true of all creativity. If someone in the room wishes to object, they must do it by building upon the idea stated. Not just pointing out its flaws.

The First Hurdle

It's quite normal for people to come back with nothing or a feeling of stasis at the first meeting. The sacred space, the empty page, can be pretty daunting and difficult. As mentioned before, lots of writers sit for hours with writer's block. It doesn't mean they shouldn't sit there.

Here is what is likely to be happening as they try and create.

When we approach 'being creative', we normally leap straight to one of these three ways:

1. risk take
2. be anarchic
3. compute, plan or architect.

Let's take deciding to play the piano using the above:

1. you buy a piano and quit your job in the hope it will make you into a professional pianist;
2. you start banging the keys until it sounds good;
3. you go to piano lessons and bore yourself with scales.

These three routes in a business setting might look like this:

1. you buy in a huge new system which costs a lot but promises to change everything;
2. you threaten, incentivise, shout 'crazy' 'blue sky thinking' techniques to staff in order to try and create an explosion of new activity;
3. you relate a huge detailed strategy broken down into a simple three thousand word action plan in order to disseminate a new approach to all.

And yes, these sometimes work through fluke or latent genius! But MOST of us will fail, feel disappointed, and feel like giving up.

Instead, encourage the team to continue their creative search without providing too many solutions or trying to lean over and start writing for them. What's more important initially for them to know is that you are....

Guarding The Space

Remember me as a penguin?

To allow creativity of any kind to be explored - be it penguins in a rehearsal room, you on a laptop writing in a shed, or new ideas in your research and development lab - you need to take a firm and committed, super-serious approach to the development and guarding of ideas. Metaphorically locking the door on the people and ideas that currently look like embarrassing fat penguins.

You must develop a defensive language that is respectful but firm, because once the idea starts to develop and people perhaps begin to be noticed as they test and try it out, the potential for interference grows and it is worth you keeping an eye on things from a distance, ready to step in and defend.

Guarding While Reviewing

Throughout their testing and their reporting back to you, there will be more and more need for you to guard the idea as it grows and its feasibility emerges.

Here's an example of how an idea might go in hospitality.

Robin's problem

You're the general manager of a hotel responsible for the various staff teams beneath you. Above you are more managers, a board, and shareholders. Robin, the manager of the cleaning team, has mentioned to you that they have an idea for how to save hours a week on the removal of clean, unused towels from rooms. If this issue can be solved, the savings will be not just time but money and the environment. You give no opinion other than enthusiasm that she has had an idea. You simply tell her to try the idea out. Get together with some people who are behind the idea, and see if she can get to a trial of some kind.

She has three other people really keen on making this work, who are all cleaners. They think that there is a way of fixing a steam cleaning box to their trolleys, which will simply sanitise towels cutting out the need to take to the laundry. One of her colleagues goes to visit a nearby hotel where they heard something similar is being done.

After some conversations Robin comes back to you and makes the case for trying it out with a budget of £200 to buy the equipment. You find the £200, or you use your contacts next door to ask the other hotel if you can borrow their equipment for a trial. You've used your power to enhance, not detract, from the idea.

The day comes for their test and as they start another manager steps in, the hospitality manager, and says, 'Oh there's a better way of doing this, we did it at my last place. We had people drop towels in the bath and...' You step in quickly. You actually had this same thought yourself, you've seen it somewhere before. But you have read this book and you are purposely NOT commenting on the actual content of the idea, you are enabling.

So you stop that manager. 'NO!' you shout in this action movie version, as you dive across the hotel lobby. 'Stand back!'

The idea needs some tweaking because they learn that the machine won't fit in the trolly but WILL fit in the.... etc etc etc... Meanwhile, what have you done? Protected and served!

What if the method that you and the other manager had seen used before, really *was* a better way of doing it? Well, I'd say that you haven't actually tried it yet: the team has no ownership over it, and you don't know it will work here. Even if it did work here, the enthusiasm of the team having made a change themselves is worth far more than a marginally better system that you introduce in a kind of 'Ace trumps King' move.

Your job is keeping things safe, enabling your staff, and assisting when essential but preferably when invited.

I've almost invariably found that, if you really allow ideas to set up and take off with the right intentions, you will very rarely reach a point of 'failure'. When ideas are owned they are important and they adapt. (The hotel could realise that this invention doesn't work for the rooms, but it works amazingly in the kitchen with the chefs who have been buying tons of tea towels...) When given the right time and space, the idea will meld into something that is intrinsic and useful - which is what the person who thought of it feels too.

At Their Own Pace

I wanted to give an example of a time when I got it wrong. Or at least, I didn't manage to get it right, but inspiration and patience did.

I used to manage someone who was sent to me at the age of 17 from another department, to be my number two in running a radio station. She was passionate and committed, first in the door, last out at night. But for years she struggled to get behind new ideas, scared of change, unable to really envisage a better way of working. And then, when I left for a career as a radio presenter, she became the boss. She visited a radio station in London that inspired her - she loved what they did and the way they worked, the music was her taste, the way they enabled kids to take part was exciting, and the methods they used instantly made her want to build something similar. She returned with a new passion for many of the ideas I had struggled to get her 'behind' for years.

It was the combination of her now being the boss and having 'ownership' over the direction of an idea, and the vision of a brighter future she could build, that allowed her to work with a new enthusiasm at the new radio station.

The station went from strength to strength, won lots of awards for 'Best Radio Station' and she now works as a producer for the BBC.

I tried everything to get her 'behind' ideas, but therein lies the problem of everything I've discussed. They were *my* ideas, not hers. The inspiration was mine, and I was trying to motivate her. Only when she found her own inspirational vision, could she drive toward it with the necessary energy - through 'ownership'. Which she did overnight with an entirely new focus and drive.

When your colleague who struggles to get behind things, finally does, it's likely to be something very close to them that feels easy. And you'll suddenly say, 'I did nothing.' You will be wrong: you exercised patience and gave time, and allowed someone the space.

HELP! We're coming up with NOTHING

What if they really are coming up with nothing and struggling? There is nothing more frustrating and sad than seeing someone stuck on their own idea.

This is part of the creative process. Whilst writing this book I have sat in a dizzy stupor, completely locked into my own thoughts and plans, unable to make the changes I wanted. But you have to allow that time in the sacred space in order to get to the other side of it.

HOWEVER, I also think there are some really good tips you can pass on to people in this position which, again, are NOT about them or their idea - but about the process. (Once again, we are not helping or commenting on the actual content of their idea or the individual who's created it, but the enabling their process of discovery.)

These are ten incredibly simple techniques that come from hyper-creative people and they work.

I.   <u>Google 'creative process'</u>

I'm not precious or have any favourites, and there are a LOT of different theories and suggested methods for breaking down the creative process. The first two that come up are a five and a seven step breakdown. Now, some of those overlap with what you've done as a manager above, and the steps are more concerned with the 'business case' end of things, which your staff don't have to worry about.   But if they are stuck, using an internet search is an easy thing to recommend - because often looking at these things even briefly can jiggle a thought loose from the subconscious and start a ball rolling. Don't be prescriptive about which sites to use, just allow them to find some - the most useful thing to someone with 'writer's block' is often just knowing that lots of people go through it - and that's sometimes enough to relax the mind into focussing on what the point was in the first place. Let them enter the internet world of that kind of thinking and see if it works for them.

2.   Use a notepad for notes!

Quite simply, this is having an open mind, being aware and spotting things as they arrive. Having for yourself, or advising others to have, a single notepad or a single 'note' in their phone for 'ideas' is simple, practical and effective. Your phone is always there, you can reach for it, scribble a fleeting idea down. It's how lots of songwriters, including Paul McCartney, work. Scribble things down when they come to you, knowing that they can then be opened and given proper thought at the right time - i.e. in the Sacred Space.

Teaching people about the three categories of project - Technical, Adaptive, and Passion, and encouraging them to 'triage' their own ideas can help too. This may be especially helpful when a complex idea they are working on has multiple facets. In other words it's highly likely that within one idea, there could be smaller problems that are adaptive or technical. This will help you to prioritise or decide how much time to allocate to each one.

3.   Listen to what people are saying

Advise them to listen carefully to what people are saying about problems within their idea. What sounds like a 'moan' about something is often a genuine statement of a problem.   Rather than try to avoid or circumnavigate the sticking points, make them focus on them, asking the person instigating the thought to consider spending some time on solving it. Again, this may bring up a variety of Technical or Adaptive problems which is why, at this point, it's good for them to know the difference. There may be useful targeted time to spend solving a technical problem and expecting a result, but if it is adaptive they may or may not find the answer, and lots of time could be spent leading to disappointment. Knowing that it may lead to feeling like it was a 'waste of time' is useful in order not to blame themselves and bring down their enthusiasm. Adaptive solutions are simply often harder.

4.   Create an honest feedback system

In their research or in the process of talking to others, they may find a certain level of wanting to guard, or be cautious. People often lie about the root of a problem because they don't want to cause offence or don't want to be seen to rock the boat. One way around this is for them to create some kind of honest feedback system.

Allowing an anonymous expression may unlock some hard truths but also some real areas to address. Inviting anonymous comments is often the best way to get honesty. Yes, you might also get gripes and nastiness - but it's your job to sift through them before sharing.

One quite radical example of this is in the Disney Parks organisation, which has an anonymous answerphone to all the top managers. Any employee can call a number and leave a message if they feel that any manager is breaking the rules. Yep. Harsh. It's an inbuilt snitch system! But it's also a lifeline to allow bad practice to be investigated. Of course people could abuse it, but the top managers will be aware of that, and bear it in mind when weighing up the suggestions.

I prefer the idea of a simple, anonymous suggestion box, to be used by a team during the development of an idea. Earlier I pointed out why I don't think they are great for initial project suggestions. They can, however, be useful when a team is engaged and needs to be unafraid of honesty during iteration.

5.   Set a timer

The Pomodoro Technique, first devised by Francesco Cirillo in the late 1980s, is well known and effective in generating creative ideas. Quite simply, encourage them to work within their space on small focussed tasks that are based on time rather than 'quality of work'. The Pomodoro Technique works like this: set a timer for twenty five minutes and bash out an attempt at whatever you're trying. You completely disregard any idea of quality whatsoever. It's like saying, 'We are GOING to paint this wall in twenty minutes; the colour and quality of the painting doesn't matter - we just have to find paint and do it.' Same with an email, a book, or screenplay - if you don't know how to begin to compose it, you can reduce the indecision by removing the need for it to be any good at all - never mind perfect. Nobody in the room is judging anyone else because it is simply known that we are metaphorically throwing paint at the wall quickly.

Then take a break and come back to the project in another twenty five minutes. You set a new goal, another twenty five minute timer is started, and you dash to do the next thing. Which might mean repainting the whole wall, or touching it up to make it more perfect, who knows. The point is that it's a game based on time. And it stimulates action.

6.   Use A Different Place

Whilst the 'sacred space' might normally be in the same meeting room, changing the environment can be a really good piece of advice for them. Try suggesting that they go somewhere different, perhaps more informal.

I remember a staff meeting I once had where we drove around Knowsley Safari Park while we came up with new ideas. It was perhaps one of the most successful meetings I've ever had. Whilst people's brains are excited about being somewhere new - looking at monkeys - their subconscious can work away at new ideas and provide lots of unexpected results.

But the same goes for you as an individual. If you really need to get something creative done, and time is of the essence, try changing your environment - for example, walk the dog around the block, and use the voice notes in your phone like a dictaphone to record your ideas until something good occurs - as in the Pomodoro Technique. That's how I started this book. I talked to myself while walking myself around the block. I don't have a dog. I began by saying, 'What is creativity?' and ultimately I didn't go home until I got angry enough at myself, and cold enough in the December air, to say, 'Every job you have done has enabled other people's creativity - so talk about that.' I had the idea for the book and could then construct what I wanted to say in it. There is no way that I could have come to the same conclusion just spending the time writing words down and hoping they formed an idea. A walk, a bath, a train journey, the toilet, at the cinema - somewhere different can really remove all the pressurising forces and subconscious messages in your mind, like, 'This is important work! Now come up with something great!'

A senior Further Education college manager once told me about a staff development initiative he fought for in his college. Traditionally the end of term in the summer would involve staff working on schemes and planning for next year. Each department did its own thing and when it came to sharing staff or option modules across different departments, territorial boundaries always caused friction between staff. So one year the principal was persuaded, after much resistance, to allow staff from across the college to mix on that staff development day in a programme of fun activities - outdoor and indoor pursuits where they worked together in teams from a menu of activities of their choice. It worked a treat; staff got to know each other and understand better their concerns about working with others from a very different subject discipline. The result was that future collaboration across the college on a wide variety of topics was made so much easier and more productive . They had been invited to devise the menu themselves and which options would be available. All the senior managers did was to agree to the staff development day being so different.

7.   The Sprint

This is a simple idea, particularly good when addressing technical problems. The essence lies in speed - putting time limits on exploring an idea, iterating, testing and developing - ultimately perhaps even launching it.

Ultimately it is like saying, 'We don't leave this room until we solve the problem.' Everyone sprints and tries to beaver away until it is solved.

It can work incredibly well for things that never seem to get done. There are countless things in any organisation that everybody knows and nobody does anything about. Like a squeaky door. 'Oh yeah, that door squeaks.' Nobody fixes it, they just spend their time telling others about the squeaky door.

Beyond the squeaky door, there can equally be benefits in considering broader issues. Give yourself sixty minutes to not just conceive of an idea, but deliver it and make it happen.

But a big NOTE here: this works best with *technical* problems. Getting everyone together and forming a detective hunt for a solution, that you know is out there on the internet or phone, is great with technical problems. 'Ok we know we have to do this, we keep avoiding it, so let's do it now. On your marks, get set, go!' But if you try to do this for *adaptive* problems, the sprint could well do a lot of harm by not being able to find the answer. There's nothing more demoralising than a sprint that leads to nothing and everyone leaves after a deadline has passed, feeling dejected.

8.   'Do one thing really well.'

Comedian Peter Kay said this to me, and his international and enduring professional success undoubtedly shows that he knows what he's talking about! It's really good advice to offer to someone who is struggling, in order to try and help them boil down to their main strength, passion, or enthusiasm. 'Why did you want to do this in the first place?' is another question that will bring them closer to that centre because often the answer is a statement of the problem they saw, followed by why they were passionate about fixing it in the first place.

Knowing the processes that you're good at allows you to make best use of your knowledge, and - in a nice way - 'stay in your lane' or 'stay in your most productive lane'. The handy thing here is that what people love doing is usually what they're best at. So don't think you must spend days trying to force yourself or others to learn new skills: allow them to flourish by allowing them to do what they love, allowing their natural ability and talent to take control.

9.   'Play the work not the occasion'

This is a useful piece of advice if your Sacred Space workers reach the point of a presentation, business case, or higher-pressure environment where they have to communicate their idea to others.

A big part of innovation is found in the moments when you have to convince others of what you're doing or what you've done. Focussing on the work rather than the occasion means that you can move your attention from the nerves felt, or the eyes upon you, and put it instead on the reasons you are passionate about what you've done. At this moment you (or your team) have spent hours within a certain world, and remaining calm and focussing on their confidence within this work will help them better answer questions or find ways of explaining what the work is and why it works. Ultimately if you are the expert, and remember that, you will ultimately retain the authority avoiding floundering.

9. 'If it can't be done in one minute it's too complicated'

This piece of advice is a slight tongue in cheek exaggeration but, generally speaking, once something has actually been created it is good to check how easy it is to use.

Let's say you and I spend six months creating a system, and within all of that time we have surrounded ourselves with the logic and reasoning within it. Let's imagine it is a computer system and, compared to what we started with, we have got it down to a simple process that involves filling in a form online. However, in order to fill in this form we have to first know how to click through five different buttons, and then add an 'asterisk' before we enter the data. Compared to what we experienced in making it, or what we started with, we might know that this is infinitely easier. However, we might be missing the fact that a brand new user doesn't have that 'generational history'. They won't appreciate the five clicks and the asterisk. They will find it frustrating.

So the final check of something is to really look at it anew, and ask if it can be used really easily.

Think about your banking app on your phone. How frustrating is it if there are more than two stages to paying someone? Even worse, if the app requires updating before you use it, or if you have to go across the house and find your PIN device and your credit card. Often these things amount to mere seconds of our lives, but that's how easily we are now frustrated. The one thing you don't want in anything you create is a complex or frustrating system.

Check your own super intelligence, and aim to make something that even a five year old could use. Whatever sector or career you've worked in the most, you'll have a bunch of 'logic' that is second nature to you but completely baffling to a layperson or an outsider. In some circles this is called 'user acceptance testing'. The user is ultimately the person who can say whether it works or not.

Make things as simple as possible, because ultimately it will create the space needed for others to live and breathe within. Only then will it become their thing.

10. Take part in one of my ideas workshops...

A quick shameless advert, because this is the right place for it...if you want to experience, personally some of my suggested techniques to create new ideas every day, based on people's passions. I'm happy to do that with you. We'll both follow my advice by creating the time and space for this (see below...) So get in touch!

A Quick Note on Notes
Why less can be more

For the most part of this creative process I have repeatedly urged you to avoid giving your own judgement. Of course there are some 'notes' that have to be given because people may be heading in a direction that is unsafe or simply a costly dead-end.

I just want to give a couple of examples to show that I empathise completely with this idea of saying less, and where I learned the importance.

At university, I worked as Assistant Director on a theatre production. The Director and I would watch a run through of a play and make notes on changes. It used to frustrate me to death that he didn't give the actors all the notes we'd written down. In later life I realised the importance of giving people just one thing at a time to focus on and get right. Flooding people with changes simply removes the ownership from them and makes it a struggle. You've been there when a manager micromanages something you're doing and it's never right, they're never happy. You blame yourself; but it's actually their fault for removing the parts of the vision belonging to you.

Once, I was asked to give a talk to all local BBC radio editors from the north of England about managing talent. I made this point and one boss asked me, 'But what DO you do about the other seventeen notes because they need to hear them?' My answer was, 'They don't. You're not being paid to make notes and give them all. It's your job to enable everyone else to do *their* job! So try to keep your mouth closed 99% of the time and see what happens.' I stand by that advice, and have seen it successfully used in action many times. But I also know it's extremely hard to understand for some. But let's be clear: if someone is doing fifteen things that are dangerous, breaking the law, harming themselves or others, or directly causing the organisation damage then of course they need to be told all of them.

Likewise, if you are working to an immediate deadline that requires a fast answer and there is a huge list of things left to do, then yes - by that point you're in crisis mode and it's time to get behind a plan and execute it.

However, in most cases of offering helpful critical advice, the manager scratching all of their itches at once usually has the negative, knock-on effect of removing ownership from the individual.

Here are three types of staff member that you might find the above technique difficult to imagine working with.

A)   Arrogant, knows everything, doesn't want to listen.
B)   Eager - so eager to please, wants constant feedback, needs support almost to the degree they are scared to think for themselves.
C)   Silent, retiring, likely to keep their thoughts to themselves even if suffering and struggling. Unlikely to ask for help.

In every one of those cases less is still more. I've seen it time and time again.

The arrogant one being given one note and told to come back is really being allowed to go away, prepare their case to present, and return to impress us. At which point they can learn from the reaction of the people they are presenting to. If you were to have given them notes throughout, it's more likely they will cherry pick or conflate things you have told them in order to blame you. 'You told me to put that bit in. I knew it was rubbish!'

The eager person really, really *wants* notes but what they really *need* is to learn that it's ok to discover things for themselves. It's great to be there for them and support the person in removing their anxieties, but giving lots of advice actually just *feeds* the anxieties; it doesn't help them. You end up with a missed creative opportunity. I've seen actors and presenters who love lots of notes, and they never manage to find their true 'swagger', their confidence, their originality. They try to please others so much that they are never truly 'dancing like nobody's watching', and that's how competent you want everyone to feel in what they do. Being given a single note and then being sent off to 'consider' a direction can be scary but also useful in terms of their ownership.

Finally the silent type. The problem here is that they won't come and ask for help. It's a tough one because I really don't like people offering unsanctioned advice (although I probably do it all the time). But here the game is not about getting them to seek advice: it is about getting them to open up - to 'show their work'. There is a common creative route I find in some people, which is that they want to create something finished and perfect before they show it to anybody else. By the time they show it, it's often right before a deadline, and it's too late to make any really simple and glaringly obvious changes. It's a shame, and it comes out of utter fear. So the trick is to keep an eye out for them, encourage them to show their work or share their thinking, and pass no judgement, just encourage them. 'Thank you for showing me, it's great to have a window into what you're doing.' If they ASK for your opinion then give it. One piece at a time.

PART FIVE

Creative Epilogues

--- Failure. What
is that?

--- How to resist
'fate'

--- Dealing with
inevitable
Frequently Found
Questions

--- You can't win
them all

--- Protego Maxima!
Again...

Introduction

A scientist friend of mine, educated in the UK but having spent most of his career in a prestigious research centre in the USA, once told me that when he reflected on his school science education, he singled out that the biggest drawback in his view was that students were taught that scientific experiments must succeed. What was missing was that students were never taught to accept that 'failure' was a key component of the route to success and that failure happened most of the time.

Failure really is 99% of creativity - if you look at it as failure. If you watch somebody trying to get a basketball in a net from the opposite end of the court, and they miss 99 times and then get it in once, you don't say they're a failure - even if statistically they have 'failed' most of the time.

But we do tell ourselves we are failures much too quickly. For all the reasons you've now read about, enough times.

The power of the very idea of failure is so strong that it can cause people to walk out, quit, have a tantrum, cry, or never even start at all.

As part of being a creative manager, you will experience what looks like failure ninety nine times out of a hundred. Reacting to it becomes a skill, and when you get that basketball in once, and get named the most incredible trick-shot basketball star, it will make all the other ninety nine times worthwhile.

Creativity is, by its very nature, made up of challenges. Which we all know means 'problems'. Creativity is joining - and even inventing - dots to solve these problems. So we can't expect to be problem free. Of all the creative challenges I come across, I just want to end with two chapters that sum up a) a common problem and b) a bunch of frequently found creative issues in the workplace.

The Creative Dead End: Waiting for A Sign

The most common and most depressing thing I hear from people around innovation is the excuse that they are somehow waiting for a sign. They are waiting for things to be 'right'. They procrastinate endlessly with lots of reasons why the universe is telling them it's not quite the right time to start the idea they are working on. The following is a great quote that I really want to say to them - but I can't because they really believe they are unique in their reasons to not move forward, and would probably punch me for insulting their feelings and beliefs.

"Rarely are opportunities presented to you in a perfect way. In a nice little box with a yellow bow on top. 'Here, open it, it's perfect. You'll love it.' Opportunities - the good ones - are messy, confusing, hard to recognise. They're risky. They challenge you ."
Susan Wojcicki - YouTube CEO.

Beliefs can be huge motivators for people of course. But relying solely on a belief that everything will be sorted by fate with no effort on your part is such a fraught strategy.

It's very possible that you feel like this sometimes, or that some members of your team never quite 'start' their action. There is little you can do to help.

One thing you certainly *shouldn't* do is make them feel bad or try and point out that they are standing still in misery. Guilt is a terrible motivator of creativity. Don't blame yourself for NOT doing something. If you decide to sit on the couch like I do every night and not go running, don't feel bad about it. You wouldn't cry over the death of someone who never existed, so don't feel bad about not creating something. You don't know whether it would have been any good anyway!

Blaming fate for either your action or your inaction is a futile pursuit. It is your choice to DO and your choice to NOT DO.

There is only one piece of advice I can share to get someone, or yourself, out of this dead end. Don't wait till you think it's the *perfect* time to develop your *perfect* idea. Here's a real life story to illustrate why...

My neighbour, let's call him Phil, has talked about starting his own shed building company for years. He also has a bad back. He also has a different reason - that he is busy every month of the year - and the years roll on, and every few months a chat about starting a shed building company happens over the fence.

Then, once upon a time, my wife and I were suddenly let down by a shed company who we had paid for the delivery of twelve rabbit sheds. (Yes, even though we had a man who wanted to start a shed company next door, he still didn't jump in to offer to make our sheds.)

We found ourselves with a truck load of wood - pieces of our sheds which had been half made, that we managed to salvage from the company on the day they went bust.

I pulled up the hastily hired truck in front of our house and asked Phil to come and have a look and give me his advice. He looked, scratched his head, and told me how f*&*&&* we were. I asked him if he would help me build them in exchange for money, and he shook his head and said he was really sorry but he was just not sure he could do it properly, and was quite busy - and he has a bad back.

I said to him, 'We have bookings in these sheds in two weeks. We have no option other than to build these sheds in the next two weeks. We need to buy loads more wood, put it together, and I have no idea how to even start. Will you PLEASE help us?'

He shook his head again. I offered money - again. He still looked unsure. Then he saw that I was about to break down and cry at the situation. I said, 'Phil, this is it - you are all we have. You're our only hope. I swear to you, if we do this and it collapses, I won't blame you, I'll just be glad we tried. Come on Phil, we can do this, help me. Help me please.'

He said, 'Go on then.'

What followed was two weeks in boiling hot sunshine putting together about twenty meters of sheds from scratch. Phil was an absolutely genius. He was precise, brilliant, a great teacher; he did everything to perfection. Almost to the point that it makes me furious now that he nearly said no!

And that's the point. Often perfectionists, or the perfectionist within us, is the reason we don't act. What was needed was essentially an absolutely desperate situation, right in front of him, that meant his humanity made him get over his perfectionism and procrastination.

Humanity wins in the end. And a touch of 'they who dare, wins'.

Frequently Found Creative Questions

What if your timescale is tight - your team is taking too long to problem solve and months go by impacting profits or targets?

Many managers feel this way about a team or an individual and in most cases this is when they are trying to do the right thing by allowing time and space but the team returns with nothing. First, they are working on an adaptive problem - trying to find a new answer and failing. And failing is not a good feeling! Secondly, it's likely that if the manager feels this way, they have answers themselves and are itching to reveal them (but are perhaps not doing so, out of trying to allow people the kind of space I've been writing about).

However, the method in this book is much more conducive to a proactive project and a deadline like this is *reactive*, to a problem that already exists. I think in these cases the staff are probably hoping, if not praying, for you to put them out of their misery and just tell them what to do.

Creativity doesn't tend to emerge as a result of pressure. But there are things you can try.

Ask the staff what the 'why' is. 'Why do you want to solve this?' Or even better 'Why did you fall in love with, or enjoy this subject in the first place?' You can often dig down into their playful or fun mind by asking this, which may shake loose some passions and turn the project into something enjoyable.

Ultimately, however, you may wish to offer them a 'big red button' - 'Go away for one more week and see if you can solve this. If not you can just push the big red button and ask me to make a plan for you.'

After you've done this and the problem solving is under way you can rest, knowing the mess is being cleared up and focus instead on new ideas, with less pressure.

What if time is tight and it's just too hard to find the time to work on new ideas?

Well, maybe you can't. But once reactive problems start to get solved, if you can start to carve out even an hour a month to work on new things, you will find over time that more space is created. Essentially when you start to work better and more productively, you are able to do more of that kind of work and less of the 'busy' work. Essentially when you make hard things easier, time is saved. But it just won't happen unless you allocate time to things that don't exist - which takes real discipline and really strong guarding.

If a member of staff just can't be motivated - they are just miserable or have done the job for so long there is no passion- can anything be done?

The only thing, after trying all the kinds of things I've mentioned, and failed (beyond firing them) is to recognise that they have chosen to be functional. They may even be happy as a cog in a machine and have no urge whatsoever to do anything beyond successfully complete their list of tasks. I'd say that even if they can't see it themselves, you will be able to notice which tasks they enjoy more than others, and it would be kind to try and employ them in areas which can best make use of those skills or interests. Over time their disposition may change so that they have more enthusiasm for doing new things.

What if someone's ideas are simply awful?

Ask them to try them out, if it's safe to do so, and let them see that they don't work. Be ready with the positives to draw from the experience even if just to say it had been a worthwhile experiment, and to encourage them to try something else that they feel enthusiastic about.

What if I ask colleagues on my wavelength to help with something and I give them everything they need, but they just don't give it their all?

Well, the hard, horrible truth is that you've probably done too much. Teachers find this A LOT. 'I've given them everything they need, told them how to do it, and they just won't!'

Usually this is just down to you being super keen on an idea that you've formed. It's yours. So you have to do the work I'm afraid. Some people love instruction manuals, but ultimately, I believe that most people prefer to feel that they've formed the idea themselves. Ownership is everything. If you've done half the work before they start, they are just contributing and don't have the same passion as you to invest in it. The teachers who teach best are often the ones who start the students from zero with a problem and let them figure out the route to solving it themselves. A good friend of mine is a primary school teacher who had to teach children about climate. He set up a problem - 'Someone is stuck on a mountain and we have to save them. What do we do?' In the process the kids found themselves getting to grips with altitude and weather and he was able to facilitate them learning about these things when they thought they were thinking primarily about helicopters and first aid.

So even if you know the answer, how you allow others to find it will help a lot in how you give them ownership and buy-in.

I have advised (literally, as an 'enterprise advisor') lots of clients to help them turn a small business idea or hobby, into an income. I could give you fifty examples of when I have given them advice that I know, for a fact, will work for them, but they have not taken it on. They stick to their other plans. It is very hard for people to get excited about what is in somebody else's head - someone else's vision. The route I try to take is to allow people, through clues, to find that vision for themselves and therefore realise and own the best route.

It's ultimately very hard to do, and takes some effort, but if you can figure out how to get others as excited as you, then it's worth the time and energy.

What if you create something great and it just isn't adopted by the business or the customers?

Then you have created something great. It's a shame that it won't be adopted but move on to the next thing, or make a phone call to someone in another organisation who might like to use it. Giving your gift of creativity away for free often comes back in some positive way. Even if it's not where you had hoped.

You need to accept that you can't win them all. When I was a 21 year old theatre director I found myself in charge of a huge responsibility. A national tour of a play with a cast full of people at least twice my age and lots of experience. Many of them surely saw me as young and naïve. Those who put their ego to one side and trusted me had a great time. Those who didn't want to listen to me, either found themselves very frustrated or simply carried on with the status quo.

One actor I was directing was delivering a speech in a strange, I thought emotionless, way. After some time, and at my instigation, we had a good chat. It turned out that he had never read the book that the play was based on but he had watched an old film of it. I realised that he was copying the tone exactly from the way the actor did it in the film. It was like an impression. It was uncanny.

I worked with him on the speech, line by line, and helped him understand the emotion and the way he could connect with the audience much more if he just forgot the movie and connected with the emotion in the scene and the writing.

124

He performed the speech for me and it was so powerful I almost burst into tears. There were two others in the room who agreed it was one of the best things they'd ever seen him do. That night he went on stage in front of an audience, and he reverted exactly to the way he'd always done it. He had created something exceptional that only three people would ever see.

Whether your idea happens once and then fails because of people not getting behind it, or whether it takes off, you can still take comfort in knowing you did it. Because ultimately a key joy of being creative is in the act of doing it. Of seeing something appear that you have never seen before.

If you create something new, even if for a moment, you should be proud and happy that you did it. The rest is the river taking away your raft, and you can't expect to control that, even at the best of times. You can only hope to give in to it, and try to steer to the bank. If you do, it's a lovely bonus. Either way, you'll be onto the next thing soon anyway.

What if you are in an organisation with command and control or a bad boss?

The top boss of a company almost always sets the tone for everything beneath. Some of the nicest people can turn into feared and hated managers when having to operate beneath the directives of a cruel or thoughtless person.

Someone said to me recently, 'You don't get to the top without being ruthless.' Actually that's not true. There are ruthless or hard decisions; for example, - 'We either lose 20% of our staff or we are unable to pay our taxes and 100% will lose their jobs' - we have to be ruthless in taking that decision. If you have to put a pet to sleep because the vet says it's time, that's pretty flippin' ruthless in your scheme of things!

What we really mean by ruthless, though, is often 'cruel'. Mean, cruel, petty, cheating. And this really does exist in some top management. But it is not ubiquitous and definitely not a prerequisite for success. What you tend to find is that people who are like that, were ALWAYS like that.

Just this week I spoke to a man and a woman who both worked with the same person, who we'll call 'X'. The man was older and had worked as a colleague of X thirty or forty years ago! The woman works under X as a boss now. Both of them had only awful things to say about X. X was a vile, cheating bully right from the start, with zero taste, using only the worst, most cynical routes to a profit. This person once openly said at a meeting 'I'm a fascist' as a badge of tongue-in-cheek but all-too-serious honour. And now person X is the boss of a large company which is gradually in decline, having made decisions of bad taste, adapting too slowly, terrifying workers, and losing all the most inventive humans - the assets!

It's just not the case that people turn bad when they become bosses. Many people in fact mellow with age. Become a little wiser. So think about your work colleagues and ask yourself what percentage of them are vile, horrible, evil people. I bet it's very few. But if the top person doesn't have an imagination they are unlikely to encourage it in others. Sometimes, creativity is almost impossible because the top boss is simply not creative. Sadly, your choice then becomes whether to stay and feel aggrieved, or leave and work somewhere else.

Often, though, there is a language they do understand - maybe money or targets of some kind. If you can package your creativity to look like it's helping those bottom lines then there is still hope. And wherever you work, or if you're in a prison cell scratching paintings onto the wall, there is always hope and a place for creativity within you.

Reveal your work from the creative space at the right time - i.e. when it's really going to be able to speak in the language they understand - which might be ego, or money.

What if I am inundated with new ideas/I work in a place where ideas come thick and fast and I have to react much quicker with judgement?

Well, either you're already in a 'hyper-creative' business and this book has been wasted on you, or you need to make it clear that there are only X number of hours your team can work on new ideas, and form an orderly queue as to who's turn it is to use that time.

Essentially while you may be using your judgement to bat away ideas you feel are lacking, you still need to recognise that there are no bad ideas. Try to avoid triaging ideas based on their apparent merit. Instead, allocate time for them to work on their idea, even if that means they have to wait a week or two to discuss it, or develop it. You don't know when a 'bad idea' may turn into a great idea. Whoever's turn it is, give them a little time to see. I've seen plenty of hyper-creative managers bypass and miss out on great ideas because they are batting them away in the cut and thrust of their daily, busy, office.

Protego Maxima!

By now, perhaps, you do understand what I was saying, with my Hogwarts reference at the beginning. Creativity really does need a protective forcefield around it.

It's well documented that when JK Rowling wrote Harry Potter she too had been stripped down to her most creative and bare self. She was going through an incredibly tough time in life, and she architected and planned and imagined and iterated this story in her own sacred spaces of trains, coffee shops and living rooms around Edinburgh. She created something incredible, not by magic, but by hard work and with the help of others.

Interestingly the 'dementors' in Harry Potter are perhaps a depiction of the depression that she has fought in her life. When you imagine a forcefield around a magical castle full of budding children with magic wands and good hearts, under attack from evil forces like depression and fascism, it's easy to understand now why I chose it as a metaphor for ideas.

We don't just shoot down ideas 'a bit soon': we do it WAY too soon and too often, and the less we do this the more happy we will be. Take that personally or in business, it is true in both cases. Just as the shots from Voldemort's army flew through the air like fireworks and bounced off the charm that was protecting the castle, so we need to protect ideas from the shots of those who don't understand that time and space is needed.

Phenomenally strong and well-meaning managers are everywhere trying, trying, trying… Instead, we need to ignite our spells of creativity. Cropping up one by one across an organisation, a town, or a family, so that gradually we are full of the illumination and protection of invention and the excitement that comes from simply loving what we are doing.

Reference from the first page...

*Lord Richard Attenborough.

He talked to my radio presenting partner, Jamie, and me for an hour instead of the scheduled ten minutes. He was the nicest man in the world, and told us about working with Charlie Chaplin, Jimmy Stewart, and Robert Downey Jr. He died shortly after. Not due to me boring him. I think. The last thing he said to us was that he loved us. The owner of Jurassic Park, and Father Christmas himself. That was the highlight of everything I've ever done. And it all happened because I decided to avoid doing a 'proper job', from birth.

Printed in Great Britain
by Amazon

61478210R00078